Along Virginia's Golden Shores

Washington
MARYLAND
Fredericksburg
Potomac River
Chesapeake Bay
Virginia
Rappahannock River
James River
Mattaponi R.
Pamunkey R.
Richmond
York River
Appomattox R.
Williamsburg
Petersburg
Jamestown
Yorktown
Cape Charles
James River
Newport News
Hampton
Smithfield
Cape Henry
Portsmouth
Norfolk
Virginia Beach
Suffolk
DISMAL SWAMP
0 10 20 30 40 50 MILES
NORTH CAROLINA

Along Virginia's Golden Shores

Glimpses of Tidewater Life

by PARKE ROUSE, Jr.

from the Newport News Daily Press
and other periodicals

DIETZ PRESS
Richmond, Virginia

Copyright 1994 Parke Rouse, Jr.

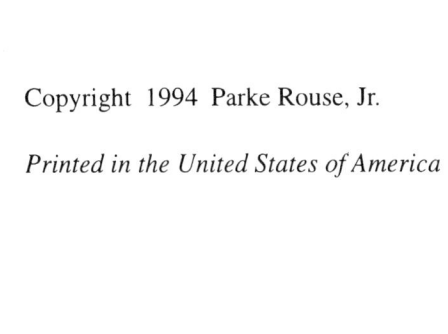

Printed in the United States of America

ISBN: 0–87517–079–X

COVER PHOTOGRAPH: *Courtesy of Virginia Tourism Development Group*

Design by Stinely Associates

For
Mary Elizabeth,
Katherine Dashiell,
and
Parke Randolph Rouse

Contents

I. THE AGE OF SAIL 1

1. Prehistoric Jordan's Point 3
2. Henry Fleete, Fur Trader 7
3. Discovering a Lost Town 11
4. On Blackbeard's Trail 14
5. Yorktown and Gloucester Town 17
6. The Story of Wolftrap Light 20
7. The Great Dismal Swamp 23
8. A Dismal Swamp Portfolio 30
9. Tobacco Fleets to England 32
10. Grist Mills in Tidewater 35
11. A Ghost on the York 38
12. Yorktown's Sunken Ships 41
13. Building New Point Lighthouse 45
14. Conflict on the York 48
15. When the British Burned Hampton 51
16. Fortifying Hampton Roads 54
17. John Tyler's Virginia 57

II. THE AGE OF STEAM 59

18. Civil War's First Shots 61
19. Burning the Navy Yard 63
20. War on the Peninsula 65
21. The Lee Family of Lee Hall 68
22. A Lone Confederate Hero 71
23. The Steamboat Age 73
24. Ships to Subdue Spain 76
25. Oysters and Violence 79
26. When Pier A Flourished 82
27. Beaches and Bathing Beauties 85
28. Storms, Hurricanes, and Earthquakes 88
29. Land of "The Life Worth Living" 91
30. Jamestown Celebrates in 1907 94

III. THE AGE OF FLIGHT 97

31. The First Carrier Takeoff 99
32. Boating Along the James 101
33. Billy Mitchell Learns to Fly 104
34. A Hard Trip to Williamsburg 106
35. The Navy's First Carrier 109
36. The Schneider Cup Races 112
37. The Heyday of Bridge-Building 115
38. Wild Beaches of Yesterday 119
39. Langley's Daring Young Men 122

40. When Prostitutes Flourished	125
41. Highways Replace Seaways	128
42. The Decline of Oystering	131

IV. THE AGE OF CITIES AND TOWNS   135

43. When Fish and Crabs Abounded	137
44. Ferries Still Ply the River	140
45. The Great Storm of 1933	143
46. Ocean Shipping Days	146
47. How They Talk in Tidewater	149
48. U Boats Scare Virginia Beach	152
49. Sending Our Boys to Fight Hitler	155
50. Discovering Alexandria	157
51. Colonial Inns Are Still Going	161
52. Those Heroic Watermen	164
53. Commuters Transform Tidewater	167
54. Where Sea Meets Shore	170
55. Saving the Marshes	172
56. Life on a Scallop Boat	175
57. Gloucester's Golden Age	178
58. Forgotten Counties, New Cities	181
59. World Fame of the Blue Crab	185
60. The Return of the Eagle	188

Acknowledgements	191
Bibliography	192
Index	193

I

The Age of Sail

Virginia Gazette

Governor Sir William Berkeley waged war against Nathaniel Bacon, Jr. and destroyed Indian's Occonneechee Town.

Jordan's Point was settled by Englishmen in Virginia's early years.

1. *Prehistoric Jordan's Point*

WHERE did Virginia's prehistoric Indians come from? How long had they lived on Virginia's shores before John Smith arrived at Jamestown in 1607?

Nobody knows the answers to those questions. Archaeologists continue to dig up evidence that humans roamed the North American continent at least 12,000 years before Europeans began their seizure of North America.

An Oregon archaeologist has taken issue with the current scientific thesis that the first North Americans were descendants of Mongols who crossed the Bering Strait land bridge from Asia to Alaska about 12,000 years before Christ

The dissenting scholar is Rob Bonnichausen of Oregon State University, who surmises from stone spear points found across the United States that prehistoric Europeans may have migrated in North America even before Mongols came from Asia.

Bonnichausen believes the prehistoric weapons—some found in Tidewater—look more like ancient European spear points than like those of the Mongols. The weapons, called "Clovis points," are so named because they were first found in ancient sites at Clovis, New Mexico.

Carbon radiation tests identify them as being 12,000 years old. That makes them the oldest man-made objects identified in North America.

Clovis points were first found in Virginia near Clarksville, on the Roanoke River, in the 1940s. There, National Park Service diggers excavated 78 Clovis points when they explored the remains of the one-time Indian trading island of the Occonneechee Indians. That was before Uncle Sam built Buggs Island Dam on the Roanoke River and submerged that romantic island of prehistory under eight feet of water.

Clovis points were fluted or striated by the prehistoric tribesmen who made them. They were then bound to sticks and used as spears or projected as arrows. In fact, Clovis points look very much like the Indian arrowheads that I and many youngsters of my generation picked up on the James River shore in the 1920s and 1930s. Ordinary arrowheads lack the fluting or striation, however.

Since those first Clovis points were dated by high-tech methods in New Mexico in 1926, others have been found in Virginia and several eastern sites. Searches by Ben McCary, a retired William and Mary professor and long-time archaeologist, and others turned up 67 pre-Indian spear points years ago in Dinwiddie County.

Recent pre-Indian finds have been made in other Virginia excavations. Such findings have increased since the federal government passed a law requiring pre-construction archaeology at sites known or believed to contain unexplored remains, either native or early European.

Theodore DeBry engraving

Algonquian Indians made life difficult for early settlers of Jordan's Point.

The 1940s dig near Buggs Island project (officially the John H. Kerr Dam) indicated that the Roanoke Valley had been inhabited by prehistoric people for many hundreds of years.

Only in 1676, when Nathaniel Bacon "the Rebel" led frontiersman against the Indians and destroyed Occonneechee Town were the aborigines driven from the Roanoke Valley. Bacon was once heroized, but recent research suggests his destruction of the Indians was cruel and unjustified.

What little is known of the Occonneechees suggests they were a long-established trading tribe which depended on exchange with other tribes for livelihood. Wrote historian Robert Beverley in 1705, Occonneechee town was the center of fur and produce trade "for all the Indians for at least 500 miles." Indian authority James Mooney called their language the trading dialect for the mid-Atlantic region, "as Algonquian was of the North, as Mobilian was of the Gulf Region, and as Comanche was in the Southern Prairies."

Judge John Tisdale of Clarksville, an authority on the Occonneechees, wrote of the nature of life in prehistoric Virginia:

> Some of these people lived here in the age in which the long-extinct mammoths and mastodons roamed the earth, and the glaciers reached down their icy fingers from the Arctic pole. Some think they retreated into this [Roanoke River] valley before the advancing glaciers of the Ice Age. Others lived here when Moses led his people from Egyptian bondage to the Promised Land, and others when Imperial Rome was mistress of the then-known world. Indeed, it appears that group after group . . . inhabited this valley during all the days of recorded history until the power of the Occonneechees was broken in 1676.

Bonnichausen, the Oregon archaeologist, believes early Europeans as well as Mongols may have migrated to North America during the last Ice Age, when lower sea levels placed Europe and North America 400 miles closer than today and when ice bridged the Atlantic between them. However you look at it, Virginia history goes back a long way.

One of the hottest archaeological sites on the East Coast these days is Jordan's Point, a peninsula in Prince George County that juts into the James River from the southern shore just downstream from the Benjamin Harrison Bridge. What started as a search for the plantation of Richard Bland has turned up evidence of prehistoric life 8,000 years before the time of Christ— one of the oldest known sites in eastern America.

More than 50 acres have been dug up, sifted and charted.

The site is a low-lying land spit first claimed in 1620 by Samuel Jordan (he pronounced it Jurdun) and acquired 40 years later by the Bland family. It was Giles Bland who in 1676 joined Nathaniel Bacon, Jr. there to launch Bacon's Rebellion against Gov. William Berkeley at Jamestown. Other Blands made their land a trading post to which Indian fur traders brought pelts for shipment to England.

In recent years Jordan's Point has been the site of an airport and a marina. The airport has been abandoned and that and adjoining land developed as a residential neighborhood. Beneath its prosaic surface, diggers have revealed its unsuspected prehistoric years as a native American settlement. The excavations were carried on by Virginia Commonwealth University with funds from the state and the National Geographic Society.

Recent digging was to uncover the brick remains of Richard Bland II's 18th-century plantation house. Two previous excavations turned up a prehistoric village site, circa 8,000 B.C., and the site of a community of Indians who lived there during what is called the late Woodland Period, around the time John Smith encountered the Powhatan Indians of Tidewater Virginia.

Most remarkable is the extent of the Jordan's Point remains. Nearly a dozen historic and prehistoric structures have been identified. The number of Native American houses found is approaching two dozen, providing a phenomenal data base for comparative research by archaeologists. The extent of the remains, the abundance of artifacts from this period, and the rarity of this type of site make this extremely valuable to researchers.

The findings at Jordan's Point have been compared to those unearthed in the 1940s at Occonneechee Island. Archaeologists searched the onetime island home of the prosperous Occonneechee tribe prior to the construction of the Bugg's Island Dam and found objects from as early as 8,000 B.C. as determined by carbon dating tests, which revealed that the Indians carried on widespread fur trade to the South.

The Jordan's Point and Occonneechee sites have something in common, for both were involved in colonial Virginia's fur trade. Most fur traders lived on the south shore of the James River, including the first William Byrd, whose trading post is currently being sought by Richmond archaeologists. Other early Southside traders were Edward Bland, Thomas Batte and Peter Poythress, all of Prince George County.

The first account of Jordan's Point was penned by an English settler in 1607. He wrote:

Virginia Division of Historic Landmarks

Fragments of an 18th century Richard Bland wine bottle have been uncovered at Jordan's Point.

"We crossed over the Water to a sharpe point which is part of Winauk [Weyanoke] on Salisbury syde. (This I call Careless Point.) Here some of our men went ashore . . . met 10 or 12 Savages who, offering them neither victualls nor Tobacco, they requited their Courtesy with the like, and left them."

The Weyanokes were one of the 30 subtribes of Chief Powhatan's confederation, and their land is shown by Smith on his 1612 map of Virginia.

Soon after Samuel Jordan settled Jordan's Point, it was attacked by tribesmen in March

1622. A fourth of Virginia's settlers were killed during this coordinated attack on settlements up and down the James River. As a result, Jordan's Point was maintained for a while as a fort, housing some 50 settlers in 22 houses.

In the 1650s, the point was owned by Benjamin and Mary Siddway, from whom Theodorick and Richard Bland acquired it. Tradition has it that Southside settlers by 1676 became so fearful of further Indian attack that they gathered at Jordan's Point and asked Bacon to lead a march against Occonneechee's Roanoke River Indians. Historians remain divided as to whether Bacon was an heroic defender of the frontier or a wanton killer of innocent Indians.

During their ownership of Jordan's Point, a half-dozen generations of the Bland family constructed four or more modest residences there. The Virginia colony also established a tobacco inspection warehouse at the point, from which hogsheads of Prince George County leaf were shipped abroad. A ferry operated across the James River to Charles City County for many years. The last Bland to live at Jordan's Point sold the land about 1900, and the property has since been divided.

No doubt other prehistoric artifacts lurk beneath the earth, and archaeologists hope to find them before the construction of buildings and highways obliterates them forever.

2. *Henry Fleete, Fur Trader*

IN THE PIONEER YEARS of Jamestown, two English boys got their names in history books by living in the wilds with Chief Powhatan's tribesmen. They were held as hostages to guarantee fair treatment of the Indians by the settlers. The best known was Tom Savage, who later settled on the Eastern Shore, and left many descendants. The other was Henry Spellman, who was killed by Potomac River tribesmen in 1622, after living peaceably with them for 13 years.

Now we learn of a third English boy who learned Indian ways in the forests of Virginia after Powhatan's tribesmen, in 1622, staged a massacre and wiped out a fourth of Virginia's 1,200 settlers. He was Henry Fleete, a young Kentishman who arrived at Jamestown in 1621 with incoming governor, Sir Thomas Wyatt. Also in the group was George Sandys, a misplaced scholar, who translated Ovid while fighting Jamestown's mosquitoes and Indians. Captured by the Anacostan Indians on the Potomac in 1622, Fleete spent five years with them before becoming a prosperous trapper and tobacco planter.

Little was known about Fleete (his descendants shortened the family name to Fleet), until his Virginia descendant, Betsy Fleet, wrote and published *Henry Fleete: Pioneer, Explorer, Trader, Planter, Legislator, Justice and Peacemaker*. It recounts the hectic career of an ambitious young emigrant, caught up in conflict with the Indians and also in land grant battles between Anglican Virginians and Lord Baltimore's Maryland Catholics.

The grant by King Charles I of part of Virginia's claim to his favorite, George Calvert, upset Virginians, who claimed Maryland land. Foremost among them was an early Hamptonian, William Claiborne, a land-grabber who had steadily patented many acres in the upper Potomac. Chief among them was Kent's Island, Maryland, now a popular yachting center.

Claiborne is best known to history as the progenitor of Louisiana's first American governor in the early 1800s, but Hampton's William Claiborne was a tough and savvy empire-builder. In Maryland, he locked horns with Henry Fleete over which colony, Virginia or Maryland, owned Kent's Island and other valuable grants.

Fleete took Maryland's side because he'd built a house early in the 1600s on St. George's River in Maryland and had become an adviser to Lord Baltimore. (The house, West St. Mary's

8   *Along Virginia's Golden Shores*

Engraving by DeBry from John White

James River Indians used log canoes to pursue fish, which were abundant in colonial times.

Manor, is still standing.) Eventually Claiborne lost Kent's and moved his family to New Kent County, where he built Romancoke plantation near the present town of West Point.

As for Fleete, after a brief sojourn in England, after his Indian captivity, he returned to the Eastern Shore and built up a profitable fur trade with the Indians, shipping beaver skins to England for hats and coats. With small sail vessels, he covered the Chesapeake and occasionally did business at Jamestown.

In 1631 he penned "A Briefe Journal of a Voyage Made in the Barque Warwick," describing his exchange to the Indians of "truck" bright cloth, metal, end mirrors in exchange for furs and corn.

Fleete visited New England and wrote of narrow escapes from Indians, in the vein of John Smith a few years earlier. At one fur-trading village, he wrote: "These [Indians] were laden with beaver and came from a town called Ussershak, where were seven thousand Indians. I carried these Indians aboard and traded with them for their skins."

In 1631, Fleete visited Jamestown to answer charges of tax violation. He was freed after trial and spent several months with Governor John Harvey, with whom he had voyaged to Virginia a

Archaeologists excavate a well near an 18th century Tidewater house site.

few years earlier.

In his coastal fur trips, Fleete lost several vessels but managed to save his skin. His travels reveal the bravery required to survive in pioneer America.

Fleete's last years of a brief lifetime were spent helping Lord Baltimore's son establish Maryland. That colony's first capital was at St. Mary's, which survives as a rustic site on a Maryland peninsula, not far from Fleete's West St. Mary's Manor. Even though William Claiborne and other irate Virginians went to court in England to protest Maryland's establishment, that colony survived.

In 1635, Fleete helped build an Indian trading post called Fleete's Hill near what is now Petersburg, to which tribesmen from Piedmont and mountainous Virginia and North Carolina brought furs. It was part of a profitable Southside Virginia Indian trading economy, carried on by Englishmen who drove through the forests westward and southward with horse trains loaded with saddlebags of truck to exchange for Indian furs.

When Lord Baltimore in the 1640s took over Maryland's fur trade from Fleete and others, Fleete returned to Virginia to live. In 1642, the Virginia Assembly granted him fur-trading rights west of the James. Then, in 1644, old Chief Opechancanough ordered a second Indian massacre, and trade was halted for several years of hostilities with the Indians. Fleete is credited with capturing the chief and delivering him to the governor at Jamestown.

On his last trip to England in 1646–48, Fleete took a wife and sired a son, Henry, through whom the Fleete family was planted in Virginia. In 1650, Fleete built a plantation in Lancaster County near Windmill Point, where he lived until his death in 1660 or 1661.

In a short life he had seen and done more than most Englishmen of his generation.

3. *Discovering a Lost Town*

LOST TOWNS give archaeologists spasms of ecstasy. On TV and in movies, we learn of National Geographic expeditions to faraway places to dig up fragments of some forgotten hamlet of long-ago times.

Actually, I'm excited by lost towns of Colonial times right here in Virginia. Jamestown was one of them until archaeologists dug it up early this century. Wolstenholme Town at Carter's Grove is another, accidentally discovered in a search for plantation out-buildings. Still "lost" is the tiny hamlet of Archer's Hope, which sprang up in the 17th century at the James River entrance to Archer's Creek, now called College Creek.

In the news long ago was Gloucester Town, which in the 18th century was a small village on the lowland portion of Gloucester Point. At one time 20 or 30 houses stood there, but after the town was repeatedly damaged by hurricanes, residents moved out.

Now comes another lost Virginia town, Queenstown in Lancaster County, on the beautiful Corotoman River. Its story is fascinatingly told by Maurice Duke of Virginia Commonwealth University. A summer visitor to Lancaster County and a sailor on the Rappahannock, Duke explains that he learned of Queenstown's existence and researched it in the Northern Neck's Mary Ball Washington Museum and Library.

Duke found that Queenstown was one of those customs collections towns decreed by the 17th-century British crown. It was duly laid out and the first courthouse of Lancaster County was placed there.

To acquire the peninsula, which is bounded by the Corotoman on one side and by Town Creek on the other, the county paid 13,000 pounds of tobacco. The seller was William Ball, whose little daughter, Mary, was later to become the mother of George Washington. In fact, the riverside promontory of the Queenstown peninsula is known as Ball's Point.

The new county paid 45,000 pounds of tobacco to Robert "King" Carter to build a courthouse at Queenstown. If you know Lancaster County, you know that King Carter was the political czar of the area, owning most of the Northern Neck. In fact, he was Virginia's wealthiest man.

Carter built the Queenstown courthouse in 1698, placing it on one of the 12 original half-acre lots of the Queenstown peninsula. The town was to be simply a double row of structures cen-

12   *Along Virginia's Golden Shores*

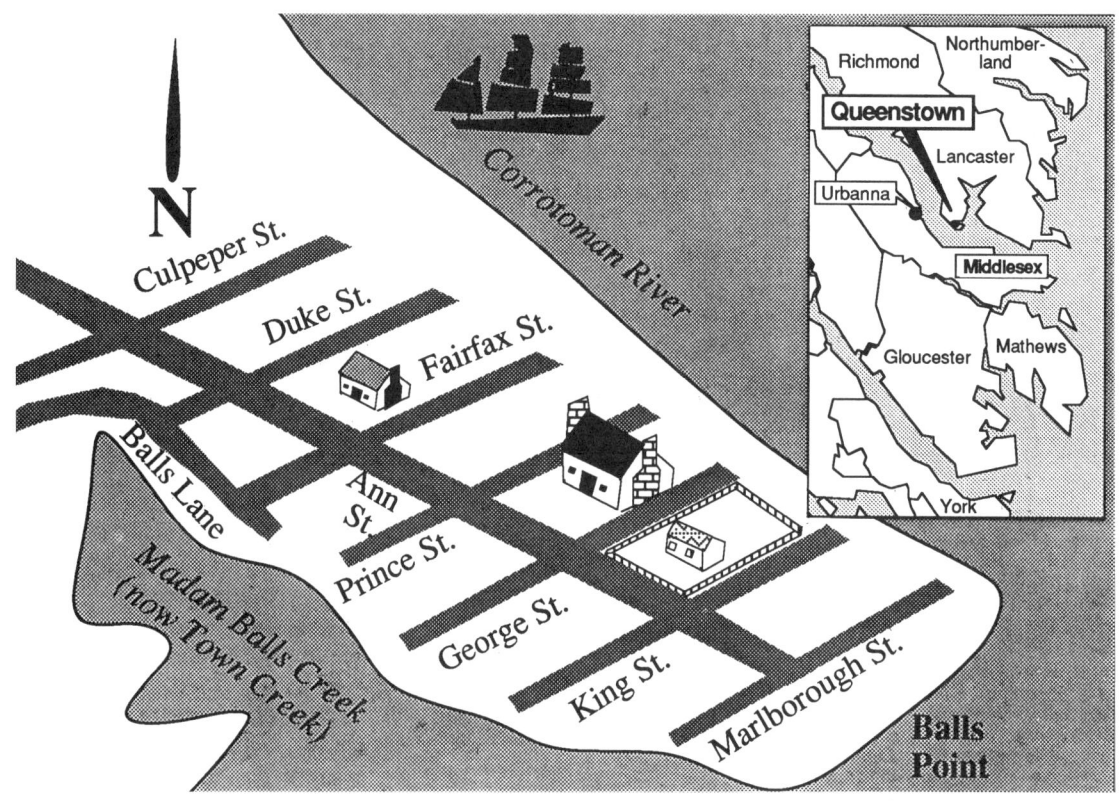

Daily Press map by Michael Asher

Queenstown was settled in early Lancaster County but abandoned by settlers after 1742.

Maurice Duke

St. Mary's White Chapel in Lancaster County is one of America's oldest churches.

tering on Ann Street. The intersecting streets were named Culpeper, Duke, Fairfax, Prince, George, King and Marlborough.

Five miles from Queenstown, Lancastrians in 1669 built St. Mary's White Chapel. It remains one of the oldest churches in Virginia, ranking not far behind St. Luke's at Smithfield, built in 1636, and the Jamestown Church, 1639. The oldest marked grave in the churchyard is that of John Stretchley, who died in 1698.

"As the small town of Queenstown grew in the late 17th and early 18th centuries," Duke writes, "half-acre lots were sold to anyone who would agree to put up a building of at least 20 square feet within 12 months following the sale." Records of 1708 show 39 people purchased lots, though few built.

Whimsically, the founders of Queenstown

decreed an annual tax of one ounce of flaxseed and two of hemp.

But as Lancaster County grew, its tiny Queenstown courthouse proved inadequate. In 1742 county citizens notifed the General Assembly in Williamsburg that Queenstown was unsuitable as a port and a town, being difficult to reach by land and dangerous to approach by water. Accordingly, the General Assembly permitted a new courthouse between the towns of Lively and Kilmarnock on what is now Route 3. It is one of Virginia's oldest courthouses still in use.

In 1754, Queenstown courthouse and jail buildings were ordered sold, but no record exists as to when the other buildings were abandoned. As happened at Jamestown after it was abandoned in 1699, bricks were removed from the decaying structures to build new buildings.

In any case, the Queenstown courthouse and houses have disappeared. "All that remains of Queenstown today," writes Duke, "is a barely visible foundation of what must have been the old courthouse." Also visible are two roadways leading to the head of Town Creek, which were probably access roads to warehouses that once stood there. But the tiny church of St. Mary's White Chapel still serves an active congregation. As one of Virginia's oldest and most unusual churches, it attracts many history-minded visitors.

Lieutenant Maynard returned to Hampton with Blackbeard's head on his ship.

4. *On Blackbeard's Trail*

IS PIRATE BOOTY from Blackbeard's day buried along the shore of the Peninsula or along other waterways in Tidewater? Over the years, hundreds of treasure-seekers have looked for pirate gold with metal-detectors and shovels, but so far as I know, nobody has yet hit pay dirt.

The legends go back to the 17th and 18th centuries when pirate captains such as Blackbeard patrolled the lower Chesapeake and its estuaries to pounce on merchant ships and seize their cargo—not to mention crew members and sometimes even the merchant ship itself.

I write chiefly of the early 18th century, when Virginia was at the height of its tobacco prosperity. That was when Edward Teach, called Blackbeard, was the scourge of the Atlantic coast. He is well remembered in Hampton, for after he was beheaded in a fierce sea battle in Ocracoke Inlet, N. C., in 1717, his grizzled head was brought by his British conquerors to Hampton and hung on a pole placed along Hampton River. The spot is still known as Blackbeard's Point.

Survivors of Blackbeard's crew were imprisoned in Williamsburg. After trial, 13 of the 15 pirates were hanged. After that, piracy never again flourished in Hampton Roads.

Piracy first appeared in the bay in the late 1600s, when the capital of Virginia was still at Jamestown. Colonists set up a fort at Point Comfort to watch for pirates and Spanish marauders, and in 1688, they caught three English pirate captains in the James River and sent them to England for trial.

The Rev. James Blair, of Jamestown, who was then in England to urge King William and Queen Mary to create a college in Virginia, persuaded the government to give one fourth of the confiscated pirate loot—a sizable amount—to help build the college. Every little bit helps.

Piracy became so bad by 1700 that the British navy sent several sloops to Old Point Comfort to combat it and to convoy Virginia's tobacco fleets each spring and fall to England. In 1700 one of the British ships engaged a pirate vessel near Point Comfort (now called Old Point Comfort), and the encounter resulted in the death of Hampton's collector of customs. The remains of his handsome but now ruined tombstone at the site of early St. John's Church, near the Hampton University campus, once read thus:

"In memory of Peter Heyman, Esq., grandson of Sir Peter Heyman of Kent [England]. He was Collector of Customs in the lower district of

James River and went voluntarily on board the King's ship Shoreham in pursuit of a pirate who greatly infested this coast. After he had behaved himself seven hours with undaunted courage, was killed with a small shot the 29th day of April, 1700. In the engagement he stood next to the Governor, upon the quarterdeck, and was here honorably interred by his order."

The pirate captain was Louis Guittar, who lost 39 of his 139 crew in the fight. The rest were hanged or deported.

But the monster of all Virginia pirates was Teach, known for his waist-length whiskers.

merchant ship he saw. If the shipmaster resisted, Blackbeard would open fire to dismast and disable the ship, then board it and seize its cargo.

For several years Blackbeard flourished, reportedly burying many of his seized treasures along Virginia waterways for later retrieval. In fact, one of his crewmen was quoted in a book, Downing's *Indian Wars,* published in England in 1737, as identifying one treasure site as being on the James River near Mulberry Island. This spot today would be near the Fort Eustis airstrip.

The information was dictated by Portuguese pirate, Antonio deSilvestro, who had formerly

English pirate Bartholomew Roberts captured vessels off the African coast in 1722.

Blackbeard is thought to have come up to the Chesapeake from the Caribbean in his fast ship manned by a crew of renegades. Blackbeard would hide in a bay or creek near Cape Charles and then rush out to pounce on any unescorted

sailed with Blackbeard and who passed the information on to a fellow crewman, John Plantain, when they met on the island of Madagascar off the coast of Africa. "He informed me," wrote Plantain, "that if it should be my lot ever to go to

Defoe's A General History of the Pirates

Virginia ships were preyed upon by Edward Teach, known as Blackbeard the pirate.

an island called Mulberry Island that there the Pirates had buried considerable sums of money in great chests, well clamped with iron plates."

Plantain identified the site as "the upper end of a small sandy covet, where it is convenient to land.... Fronting the landing place are five trees among which he [deSilvestro] said, the money was hid."

The account was reprinted in 1954 in the Fort Eustis newspaper, *The Sentinel*, and set off a wave of searchers for buried treasure. However, the shoreline of Mulberry Island has eroded over the years and it was greatly disturbed by Confederates when they built Fort Crafford there in 1862. Thus, so far as this chronicler has been able to learn, nobody has dug up the booty.

Legends of Blackbeard survive especially in Hampton, where his dismembered head was once exhibited, and at Okracoke, North Carolina, where he was killed. But he is also remembered on the Eastern Shore, where his pirate ship often hid to await combat, and at Bath, North Carolina, where he liked to live ashore and tend his pleasure garden.

Blackbeard came to Virginia from the Caribbean, where he was described as "a swaggering, merciless brute." He is said to a have started out as Ned Teach—or it may have be Thatch, Thack, or Tack—in Bristol, England. He went to sea as a hired wartime privateer and made a reputation for boldness while operating out of Jamaica in Queen Anne's War, from 1703 to 1713.

After that he turned to piracy, winning fame by defeating a British man-of-war in combat. By 1717 he had worked his way up to Chesapeake Bay on his flagship, *Queen Anne's Revenge,* and its motley crew of international outlaws. A song of the period, perhaps written by young Benjamin Franklin, reflects Americans' fascination with Blackbeard:

> So each man to his gun,
> For the work must be done
> With cutlass, sword or pistol
> And when we no longer can strike a blow,
> Then fire the magazine, boys, and up we go!
> It's better to swim in the sea below
> Than to swing in the air and feed the crow,
> Says jolly Ned Teach of Bristol.

Blackbeard so terrorized North Carolina shipping in the early 1700s that that colony persuaded Governor Alexander Spotswood in Williamsburg to dispatch two British warships from Virginia to Okracoke in 1717 to capture or kill him. After a lengthy battle, one of the British vessels closed on Blackbeard, boarded his ship, and killed the pirate chief and part of his crew. The rest were brought back as prisoners to the jail in Williamsburg, tried, and executed or punished.

After that, piracy slowly subsided on Virginia's coast.

Detail of French map of York in 1781 shows fortified shore of Gloucester Town.

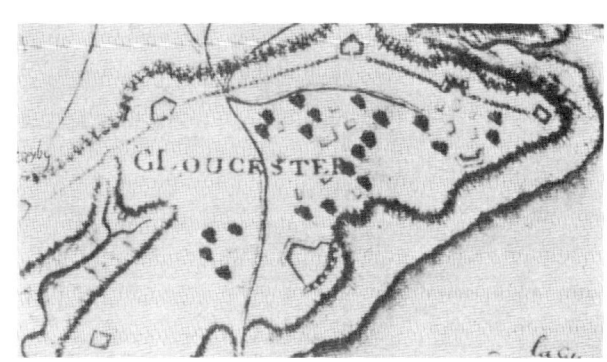

Virginia Division of Historic Landmarks

5. *Yorktown and Gloucester Point*

WHENEVER I ENCAMP on the banks of the York at Gloucester Point, I think of those days in October 1781 when the British held both sides of the river, hopefully awaiting a relief fleet sent by General Sir Henry Clinton from New York. Alas, it never came.

The focus of that siege was tiny Yorktown, held by Lord Cornwallis, but Gloucester Point was occupied by his henchman, Colonel Banastre Tarleton, the demon cavalryman. A granite marker near the point notes that Tarleton surrendered an hour after Cornwallis, "thus ending British rule in America."

For all I know, that bluff where I sit and gaze at traffic tieups on Coleman Bridge was once the campsite of "Bloody Ban" Tarleton and his horsemen. At least, that's the way it looks on a Revolutionary War field map drawn by a French cartographer during the September-October 1781 siege. After Cornwallis surrendered, the British moved out, and Gloucester slowly got back to normal.

Historic as Gloucester Point is, the National Park Service in 1931 decided not to include it in the Colonial National Historical Park. But it doesn't mean the area isn't important. In fact, the village of Gloucester Town in its infancy almost became the capital of Virginia. That was in 1677, when Virginia's executive council proposed to replace the Jamestown statehouse that Nathaniel Bacon had burned with a new one at what was then called Tindall's Point. Only a negative vote of 21–18 in the House of Burgesses defeated it.

Except for the Revolution and Civil War, the world has left Gloucester Point pretty much alone—that is, until the Coleman Bridge was built in the early 1950s. Since then the narrow throat of the York there—less than a half mile wide—has become one of Virginia's highway stress points. The bridge is currently being widened.

Gloucester Town evokes the romantic allure of other ruins, like Jamestown and Green Spring. In the *Colonial Williamsburg Magazine,* journalist Wilford Kale sums up the life of that Colonial port before it succumbed to Yorktown's competition. The site had been chosen by the Virginia Assembly in 1680 for one of Virginia's tobacco ports, but it didn't grow beyond the 47 lots shown on its 1707 town map. "Refortified Gloucester Town flourished during the first quarter of the 18th century," Kale writes. "A tobacco inspection warehouse began operation," and "by

17

Virginia Gazette

Early Gloucester Town once lined Gloucester Point, now site of Coleman Bridge approach.

1726 residents collectively petitioned the House of Burgesses to prepare a bill forbidding the free ranging of livestock." Virginia forces manning Gloucester Town's fort were ordered to withdraw when Cornwallis' army marched into Yorktown. Soon Tarleton's troops were constructing new earthworks on the point. By that time the point had dwindled to about 12 houses.

Describing Tarleton's surrender of Gloucester Town on September 18, 1781, Kale writes:

"At three o'clock the Gloucester garrison marched out, Tarleton's cavalry with swords drawn and trumpets sounding. His soldiers laid down their arms as prescribed for the garrison of York. England's claim to colonial America came to an end."

After the Revolution, Gloucester Town continued to doze. Probably its low-lying waterfront—now a public beach and Virginia Institute of Marine Science dockside visible from the

Artistic seaman John Gauntlett in 1755 depicted Gloucester Town overlooking York River.

overarching Coleman Bridge—proved vulnerable to hurricanes, as Yorktown's early dockside buildings had also proved.

Only one colonial Gloucester Town feature survives today. That's the meandering ancient road that runs through the VIMS campus and down Wharf Hill to the bathing beach. Rectangular indentations in the soil indicate ruined foundations of earlier days, but few have been excavated. Gloucester Town is now on the Register of Historic Places, and VIMS respects the designation. The Virginia Landmarks Commission plans further research at Gloucester Point. David Hazzard, supervisor of excavations for the commission, says preliminary digs have found "excellent artifacts—everything from military items to brass candle snuffer holders to beautiful Delft tiles. . . . We have only touched two areas, and they suggest that much more lies beneath the surface. We know that there has been more than 300 years of continuous occupation of the site. Because we have located that first street, we have been able to pin down a portion of the 1707 town plat."

During the 1976–82 Revolutionary Bicentennial, a Gloucester Committee under William Hargis, then VIMS director, restored the crumbled Revolutionary and Civil War earthworks at Gloucester Point, neatly bisected by Route 17. Picnic tables and the 1981 Bicentennial marker identify the area for passers-by.

Yes, it's pleasant to summer on the site of old Gloucester Town. The nearby bridge traffic I watch may grow hysterical, but it's calm and peaceful where I read in my hammock.

English merchantman Wolf *grounded near Mobjack Bay in 1691, now site of Wolf Trap Light.*

Author's collection

6. *The Story of Wolf Trap Light*

AT THE COAST GUARD Reserve Training Center at Yorktown reservists are trained in everything from rescuing people at sea to repairing navigation lights put out of commission by nesting Chesapeake Bay ospreys.

I visited the center and was surprised by today's high-tech equipment. It permits Coast Guard stations to keep in touch by radio with thousands of navigation lights, bells and buoys which direct mariners through coastal U.S. waters.

Such a navigation light is Wolf Trap, which I see every time I sail down the York and out into Chesapeake Bay. It stands in shoal water a mile or so off the shore of Mathews County, close to the main Chesapeake channel linking Virginia and Maryland. Like all the Coast Guard's modern aids, it is an unmanned device.

It takes its name from the ill-fated British ship *Wolf,* which ran aground there in 1691. The *Wolf* was inbound to protect colonial shipping against French privateers during the warfare then raging between Britain and France. The 350-ton sailing ship was one of 41 vessels sent by the British admiralty to help Virginia and Maryland tobacco shippers escort their cargo to England against the threat of French attack.

The *Wolf's* experience in Virginia nearly ended her career. The 20-gun ship, manned by 33 officers and crew, had sailed from Cornwall to Virginia in December 1690, zig-zagging her way past Cape Henry nearly three months later. Next day, while inbound from the capes to the Rappahannock, she ran aground off Milford Haven, then part of Gloucester County and now of Mathews.

Captain George Purvis, her skipper, sent ashore for help, and boats from Gloucester and Middlesex came out and tried to pull her off the sandbar. After several days' failure, her salvors lightened her by removing her guns, ammunition and provisions. At last she was dragged clear of the mud. But the strain opened up the *Wolf's* hull. Purvis noted that sea water had flowed in and "damnified most part of our bread and Peas and Flower." With difficulty, he brought the *Wolf* to a Rappahannock River landing and had her careened so he could repair damage.

The incident would have quickly passed had not owners of the salvage ships submitted charges which Purvis thought excessive. Though he admitted that "without their help, Shee must have been utterly lost," he went to court to

Shad fishing with seine nets once provided plantation's slave food, but shad are few now.

reduce their demands.

When the Virginia Assembly met at Jamestown several months later, burgesses from Gloucester and Middlesex complained to Governor Francis Nicholson that the *Wolf's* captain was trying to welch on his debts.

When the governor submitted the matter to his council, they ordered Purvis to pay them at a rate of 23 shilling a month instead of the 18 he had offered. Since the salvage ships had "performed as good and as hard a service as any Seaman could," the council ruled, they deserved prompt payment. Besides, they noted, that affair was causing "great Clamouts in the Whole Country," which could cause a "dangerous Consequence to the peace and quiett" until it was settled.

Defying the council, Purvis sailed the *Wolf* from Lynnhaven Roads with the tobacco ship convoy without paying the debt. This so annoyed Governor Nicholson that he issued an order "to ascertain the estate of Captain George Purvis" and ask authorities in England to stop Purvis' pay.

The fiery Nicholson also demanded that the sheriffs of Gloucester and Middlesex make "diligent inquire" for any property of Purvis or the *Wolf's* owners in Virginia so it could be seized by the colony.

Nicholson's proclamation noted that "many

men, Sloopes, and boates were Imprest for the [salvage] service, [as a result of] the Chearfull and Ready Endeavour of the Said men and Assistance of the Sloopes and boates many days, all the Gunns, Amunicon, provision &c were taken out of the said Shipp, the water baild and pumped out . . . Shee [the *Wolf*] gott off. . . ."

It took awhile for the salvage crews to get their money, but they finally did. On January 1, 1693, Middlesex County Court noted that William Churchill, a county official, "made proclamation that all persons which did service on board their majesties ship *Wolfe* should repair to him, and be paid for the same. . . ."

The incident gave the name "Wolf Trap" to the Mathews shoal. When John Thornton about 1695 issued his "New Map of Virginia," it showed "Wolf Trapp" not far from New Point Comfort. But the hazard remained unmarked until 1772, and in the meantime several other ships went aground there.

One was the ship *President,* which was caught there in May 1748 as she was sailing for the British Isles with 469 hogshead of tobacco. In his diary for May 31, 1748, Robert Rose noted that "Mr. James Anderson from Wmsburg dined with me, and told, the *President* was got clear of the Wolf Trap but had Damnified all her Load, 100 Hhds Excepted and that privateers infested the Bay of Chesapeak."

Finally, in 1772, the state of Virginia belatedly authorized the present Cape Henry lighthouse and marked other coastal landmarks with day beacons. Since then, Wolf Trap has had both a lightship and a lighthouse before the present Coast Guard beacon was placed there.

If you sail the Chesapeake, you regard Wolf Trap Light as a good friend.

7. *The Great Dismal Swamp*

ACROSS the Virginia Boundary with North Carolina lies the largest swamp in the United States, known throughout history as Dismal Swamp.

Today it is a Federal wildlife refuge alive with bears, deer, and dozens of other animals and birds, but in earlier years "The Great Dismal" figured largely in the timbering and fur-trapping of the infant nation.

The return of the land to the public domain was largely through the generosity of the Union Camp Company, one of the nation's biggest forest products companies. In 1973 it gave 49,000 acres—more than half the swamp's acreage—to the Nature Conservancy, a private conservation agency that acts as an unpaid middleman for the United States Department of the Interior. Other tracts of the swamp have subsequently been added.

Edgar Allan Poe and the Irish poet Tom Moore are among writers who have written of the swamp's secrets. And George Washington is among the frontiersmen who explored it. In fact, Washington long ago owned part of the acreage that the six Camp brothers of Franklin, Virginia, bought in 1899—the same land given by Union Camp to the nation in 1973.

Thought it was long ravaged by timer-cutters and by the ditches they dug to float timber out of the swamp, the Dismal is today reverting into the animal-infested wilderness it was in Powhatan's day. In its depths animals, birds, and fish can live again without threat from man. It is one of America's largest wildlife preserves, a legacy for future Americans.

The one major human intrusion into the Dismal that remains is Dismal Swamp Canal, proposed by George Washington and cut beginning in 1785 to link Norfolk by inland waterway with Albemarle Sound, North Carolina.

Over the United States' history, Dismal Swamp has piqued the curiosity of many. William Byrd II of Westover, a member of the Virginia-North Carolina survey party which in 1728 extended the dividing line between the two colonies through the swamp, wrote of it in his *History of the Dividing Line*. Washington as a young man visited the swamp six or seven times and headed a group of eight Virginians who in 1763 obtained a crown grant of 40,000 acres of unclaimed swamp land free from the Virginia government. Some 18th century European visitors to the American colonies ranked it with Niagara Falls and Natural Bridge as one of the "seven wonders" of North America.

The Camp brothers who helped create the Union Camp Corporation, grew up before the Civil War in Southampton County, Virginia, close to the swamp. As loggers after the war, they worked in it and felt its spell. In 1947 their company described itself as operating "in the center of the heavy loblolly pine timber area which joins the historic Great Dismal Swamp."

It was William Camp, the fifth born of ten children, who knew the swamp best. A wanderer in his youth, he hoped someday to own it. Fourteen years after his 1870 marriage to Texanna Gay of Isle of Wight County, he moved his family to Suffolk and started Gay Manufacturing Company, a lumber firm, with his father-in-law, William H. "Pappy" Gay. For a while he lived at the swamp's edge.

Like most of the Camp timbermen, William Nelson Camp was a daring speculator. So was his father-in-law, who in the 1880s created the short-haul Suffolk and Carolina Railroad to bring lumber and crops from North Carolina through Dismal Swamp to Suffolk. Even after William Camp moved to Florida in 1891, he kept hankering for the Dismal Swamp. In 1899 he made a down-payment on 40,000 acres, contracting to pay $76,500, or about $1.92 an acre.

Within Camp's purchase lay Lake Drummond, a large freshwater body in the midst of picturesque cypress and cedar trees. These trees chiefly attracted Camp, though he and his brothers later did even better selling the swamp's pine trees.

Bill Camp's biggest problem was how to move timber out of the swamp to lumber mills. He proposed to do this by floating logs in Jericho Canal, which had been dug in colonial times for the same purpose. Jericho Canal stretched from Lake Drummond north to the headwaters of the Nansemond River at Suffolk.

Unfortunately, Bill Camp's log removal plans upset the Lake Drummond Canal and Water Company, which needed the lake's water to feed its nearby Dismal Swamp canal. That canal had been served since its start in 1785 by a sluice from Lake Drummond, which yielded only enough water to float shallow-draft schooners through the canal. However, the canal company in 1900 announced plans to enlarge its sluice from Lake Drummond in order to raise its water level.

Promptly, big and feisty William Nelson Camp brought suit against the Lake Drummond canal company to prevent the enlargement, arguing that it would make his Jericho Canal unusable for floating logs.

The case was an historic one, raising issues hitherto undecided in a nation which had given little thought to conservation. When the court ruled against Camp, he appealed and his case went before the Fourth Circuit Court of Appeals in 1903. Again the court ruled that Camp's ownership of the land around and beneath Lake Drummond did not give him possession of its waters. The decision upset Camp, but he devised ways to remove his timber.

Twenty-six years after the history-making canal decision, the United States government in 1929 bought the Dismal Swamp Canal to become part of the nation's new Intracoastal Waterway system, administered by the Army Corps of Engineers. Congress had decided that the nation needed publicly owned inland waterways for safe coastal transport in wartime.

In 1909 William Camp, then living in Ocala, Florida, transferred his two-fifths interest in his Dismal Swamp purchase (five of his brothers owned the rest) to Camp Manufacturing Company of Franklin, repaying most of the money he had borrowed from the company for his Florida operations.

The land-rich Camps went to court a second time in the 1920s over their Dismal Swamp holdings, this time to resist a claim that their company had trespassed on others' property. Camp attorneys John C. Parker of Franklin and Toy Savage of Norfolk searched George Washington's hand-written diaries for details from his original purchase to defend their own purchase. Informed by Earl Gregg Swem, librarian at the College of William and Mary, that Washington's

George Washington once owned part of Dismal Swamp, here depicted by Currier and Ives.

diary of his first Dismal Swamp visits reposed in a New York archive, they went there and consulted it.

The mystique of Dismal Swamp goes back to prehistoric times. Lake Drummond lay undiscovered by English settlers of Virginia until one William Drummond discovered it about 1650, before becoming North Carolina's first colonial governor in 1662. After Drummond had been hanged by Virginia's Governor Berkeley in 1677 for taking part in Bacon's Rebellion, the lake for many years attracted few except for runaway slaves, who often lived as outlaws in the swamp.

Scientific knowledge of Dismal Swamp began only in 1728, when the disputing Virginia and North Carolina colonies sent their commissions to survey the area. Writing his account of the survey, later published as *A History of the Dividing Line*, William Byrd II gave it the name, "Great Dismal Swamp." Wrote Byrd, "The Dismal is a very large swamp or bogg," rich in timber but "a horrible desart" whose "foul damps ascend without ceasing, corrupt the Air, and render it unfit for Respiration. . . . Nor, indeed do any birds fly over it for fear of the noisome exhalations that rise from this vast body of dirt and nastiness." Byrd called it "a frightful place."

So dense was the area that Byrd and his 1728 cohorts spent ten days moving the survey only fifteen miles. "Never was rum, that cordial of life, found more necessary than in this dirty place," Byrd wrote. A few years later Byrd drafted a proposal for the colony to drain the swamp with ditches. Anticipating George Washington, Byrd proposed a "channel" or canal south from Suffolk via the Elizabeth and Nansemond rivers to Albermarle Sound in North Carolina.

Byrd's conception was partly realized in the

years 1785–1805, though the canal then built was inadequately engineered and impractically shallow. The United States government improved it after it took it over in 1929.

On one of George Washington's visits to the swamp he took surveyor's sights and made entries in his diary. In 1763 he became the spokesman for eight Virginians who sought the colony's free grant of 40,000 unclaimed acres, or about half of the swamp lying in Virginia. Their request to Governor Francis Fauquier was granted, and the land given to Washington, Thomas Nelson, Robert Burwell, John Robinson, Thomas Walker, Fielding Lewis, and Anthony Bacon, all Virginia landowners.

Apparently, the eight men had hoped to timber the "finest cypress, juniper, and other lofty wood," as Washington described it. However, the oncoming American Revolution prevented it.

In his diary for May 26–28, 1763, Washington recorded one visit to the swamp. He travelled there from Suffolk, noting taverns and households he visited along his horseback trip to Great Bridge, in what was then Norfolk County, now the city of Chesapeake. From there he rode to Northwest Landing in Norfolk County and thence into North Carolina. At Washington's instigation, a Norfolk surveyor named Gershon Nimmo platted the 40,000 acres for him, completing the plat six months later.

Nimmo's survey, now in the Library of Congress, was dated at Norfolk on November 20, 1763. It is the earliest depiction of Lake Drummond.

Washington's Dismal Swamp Land Company was chartered by the Virginia Assembly in January 1764, and an act was passed by the Assembly "to enable certain adventurers to drain a large tract of marshy grounds in the counties of Nansemond and Norfolk" and permit them to "enter upon and . . . make such canals" as were needed.

Twenty years later, after Washington had led the colonies to triumphant nationhood, he was still trying to profit from Dismal Swamp. From Mount Vernon in 1784 he wrote Hugh Williamson, "I have long been satisfied of the practicability of opening communications between the waters which empty into Albermarle Sound thro' Drummond's Pond [Lake] and the Waters of Elizabeth and Nansemond's Rivers."

Clearly Washington underestimated the difficulty of cutting his "channel." That was chiefly the result of inaccurate surveys, which indicated that there was less than two feet difference in the height of the swamp land from one end of the canal route to the other. Actually, the incline was much greater, eventually necessitating a series of canal locks, still in use, which greatly increased the canal's sophistication and cost.

During their 33-year ownership of part of Dismal Swamp, Washington and his colleagues had ditches dug to drain it and to float out timber. One canal, called Washington's Ditch, was redug by the Camp Manufacturing Company in the 1950s. The company's literature in those years cited Washington's experience with Dismal Swamp, reproducing a Washington letter of February 18, 1793 to Henry "Lighthorse Harry" Lee, extolling the swamp's value and attempting to sell Lee, then governor of Virginia, Washington's share. Lee agreed, but in 1799 was compelled to back out of the deal.

In his letter to Lee, Washington said he was "one of a company who took up, in or about the year 1762, all the ungranted land lying in the Great Dismal Swamp, in the vicinity of Norfolk, Portsmouth and Suffolk and offering to sell his share for £5000 in Virginia currency:

> Forty thousand Acres of the interior and richest part of this swamp has been, as the subscriber is informed, patented in the name of the Members of said Company; and probably is all they will ever obtain, altho it is far short of what they expected –
>
> This swamp in fertility of soil cannot be exceeded. It is covered with the richest Cypress & Juniper & other lofty Wood. Its undergrowth is luxurious Canes.
>
> In the opinion of the Subscriber it may be easily drained, and when drained is equal to the riches land of So. Carolina, which in its unreclaimed state sells from ten to fifteen pounds Sterling pr Acre and from thirty to fifty

when reduced, and in order for cultivation.

Its vicinity to the places above mentioned or its contiguity to the fine rivers of Nansemond and Elizabeth on which these acres are, gives the tract advantage over almost any other of equal quantity in the United States; and the Canal which is now opening from Elizabeth River to Pasquotank, a River of Albemarle Sound, passing through the same, adds invitingly to its worth. To describe all its advantages would require more time than my hurry, and the few minutes you allow me will enable me to do . . .

For the whole of this interest . . . I will take Five Thousand pounds, Virginia Currency . . .

George Washington

Philadelphia February 18th 1793

In 1803 Dismal Swamp was visited by Tom Moore, the Irish poet, who on a visit to America had stopped in Williamsburg at Bassett Hall. Moore's visit inspired his ballad, "The Lake of the Dismal Swamp," wherein a young man imagines his dead sweetheart is alive and lost in the swamp. The ballad, which recounts the youth's ghostly pursuit, became a favorite:

> They made her a grave too cold and damp
> For a soul so warm and true.
> And she's gone to the Lake of the
>   Dismal Swamp,
> Where all night long, by a fire-fly lamp,
> She paddles her white canoe.

In 1805 the original Dismal Swamp Canal, dug without the locks later found necessary, was opened to boats. It ran from Norfolk to South Mills, North Carolina, and thence to Albemarle Sound in eastern North Carolina. The 1805 company report explained:

> During this year a junction has been effected betwixt the waters of Elizabeth River and Pasquotank. . . . The canal is cut its full width [originally 15 feet] . . . . It is navigable to admit shingle flats to pass the whole distance river to river.

The reference to "shingle flats" refers to the vast quantities of cypress, cedar, and chestnut cut in the swamp and split by woodsmen into roof shingles. These three woods were especially durable and were eventually nearly all cut out in the swamp. The finished shingles were floated out of the swamp on "shingle flats," or barges. *Harper's Illustrated Weekly* artist David Hunter Strother, calling himself "Porte Crayon," visited the swamp in 1850 and sketched shingle splitters and their mule carts and laden barges, as well as a runaway slave living in the swamp.

Toll charges advertised by the Dismal Swamp Canal in 1807 were modest:

18 inch and 22 inch shingles	15 cents per 1,000
24 inch shingles	33 cents per 1,000
36 inch shingles	50 cents per 1,000
Barrel staves	50 cents per 1,000
Hogshead staves	75 cents
Carts passing the road	25 cents
Wagons passing the road	50 cents
Horse and man	12 cents
Head of cattle	6 cents
Hogs and sheep	2 cents

After the British invaded Virginia in the War of 1812 and attacked Craney Island and Hampton, the United States government felt need for internal waterways like Dismal Swamp Canal, which would protect domestic commerce from enemy ships in wartime. Accordingly, the United States in 1829 bought 200 shares of stock to encourage completion of the canal. President Andrew Jackson, who came to Old Point that year to inspect the newly built Fortress Monroe, crossed Hampton Roads to see the canal.

A New York paper described President Jackson's reception at Deep Creek:

> The Director [of the Dismal Swamp Company] and party disembarked, and a collation was immediately spread on the table, made of cypress shingles. . . . The President of the United States and other gentlemen were each provided with a clean shingle, which answered for a plate. The servants handed around the slices of Virginia ham, smoked beef, and tongues, and everyone immediately set to work to demolish a good portion of the good things so kindly provided. General Jackson said it put him in mind of the old times; that he had often taken his meals on

the log in the woods, and always with good appetite. The fresh air and exercise, he observed, were the best sauces; every thing was truly excellent.

The Virginia Assembly in 1829 authorized a $50,000 lottery for the benefit of the canal, with prizes from $60 to $10,000. Receipts paid for necessary improvements. Once they were made, a local shipper began to operate boat service through the canal from Norfolk to Elizabeth City, Plymouth, Halifax, and Weldon, North Carolina.

Map by Richard Stinely from *The Timber Tycoons*

Dismal Swamp lies across the Virginia-North Carolina line and is a wildlife refuge.

This passenger service created need for a stopover for rest and dining, which was soon met by the erection of the Lake Drummond Hotel alongside the canal, on the tow path used by mules to pull canal barges. Built in 1829, the hotel capitalized on the romantic name, Lake Drummond, and served patrons its reputedly healthful "juniper water," flavored by roots of the juniper. Built astride the Virginia-Carolina line, far from law enforcers, the hotel got a reputation for its patrons' illicit romances and illegal duels, far from the eyes of the press. Its remoteness suited fugitives from justice and eloping couples. Owner Isaiah Rogerson blatantly advertised in 1830:

> This establishment (being situated on the N.C.-Va. line, one-half the building in each state), is in a superior degree calculated to render facilities for matrimonial and duelistical engagements, and should the purchaser become a magistrate, the facilities would be much increased though rather detrimental in the latter. Indeed, it is a stand fully applicable for all the purposes of life, as eating, drinking, sleeping, marrying, duelling, &c, in all its varieties.

Although the hotel soon changed hands, it helped create a commercial market for juniper water. Woodsmen insisted that the lake's tannic acid, absorbed from tree roots around the lake, kept water palatable for long periods, even in wooden casks. Accordingly, Lake Drummond water was commonly used by seagoing vessels and served by such fine hostelries as the Hygeia at Fort Monroe. A Hygeia advertisement before the Civil War promised patrons "a constant supply of Juniper Water from the Dismal Swamp."

As bitterness mounted before the Civil War, the plight of fugitive slaves in Dismal Swamp was publicized by northern Abolitionists as proof of slavery's evils. Henry Wadsworth Longfellow in 1842 described a runaway slave, hiding in the "dark fens of the Dismal Swamp." Harriet Beecher Stowe in 1856 published *Dred: A Tale of the Great Dismal Swamp*, hoping to repeat the success of her *Uncle Tom's Cabin* five years earlier. Another Abolitionist, the Northern urban planner, Frederick Law Olmsted, in 1856 mentioned Dismal Swamp's fugitive slaves in *A Journey in the Seaboard Slave States*. He deplored their pursuit by masters with bloodhounds.

With the revival of North-South trade after Appomattox, timbering and commerce down the Dismal Swamp canal revived. Regular steamboat service was begun by the passenger and freight vessel *Fox* in 1865, later taken up by other steamers. Like other river boats and canal boats in this period, Dismal Swamp packets connected with larger vessels and with railways at Norfolk, Portsmouth, and Suffolk, offering service through Chesapeake Bay to Atlantic ports.

After the Civil War, busy timber crews cut out much of the remaining juniper, cedar, and chestnut in Dismal Swamp. Besides the Camps, other timber operators were Baird and Roper, two Norfolk partners who had fought for the Union in the Civil War and remained in Virginia afterward. The firm became the largest lumber mill in Norfolk and emerged into the John L. Roper Lumber Company until absorbed by Norfolk Southern Corporation.

Dismal Swamp offered fine hunting, and most landowners there permitted friends and employees to hunt there despite the danger of setting fire to the woods. Camp Manufacturing Company permitted more than 30 hunt clubs to build cabins around Lake Drummond during its ownership of swamp lands.

A common practice in Dismal Swamp was the digging of lumber ditches to permit the removal of timber, later recognized as destructive. Deep ditches were cut to float heavy logs, while shallow ones were cut to drain off surface water and provide a footing for lumber cutters. In the 20th century, mechanized equipment was developed to expedite ditch-digging. The town of Portsmouth about 1908 dug the extensive Portsmouth Ditch to help provide the city with Dismal Swamp water.

Extensive logging and ditching slowly changed the swampy character of Dismal's wetlands and threatened many species of flora and fauna. By the time of World War II, conservationists were concerned. They complained that lumbermen were draining the swamp's life blood. After Rachel Carson's best-selling *Silent Spring* seized America's consciousness in 1962, concern for America's swamps and forests grew.

In view of the need for forest conservation, the Union Camp Corporation in 1972 decided to deed its Dismal Swamp lands to the nation, hoping its example might lead other to make similar gifts. By this time the 40,000 acres the Camps had bought in 1899 had been increased to more than 49,000, forming a large rectangle from Suffolk southward to a point below the North Carolina line.

The Union Camp Corporation—successor to the Camp Manufacturing Company—announced its gift to the nation of February 22, 1973—George Washington's birthday. At ceremonies at the Department of the Interior in Washington, the gift was received by the Nature Conservancy, a private conservation agency acting as an unpaid middleman for the Interior Department. It was the largest corporate land gift in American history.

The Federal government permitted Union Camp to deduct the property's appraised value —$12,600,000—from its taxable earnings. This added about $6,300,000 to Union Camp's net income that year.

Today, operated as a Federal wildlife refuge, Dismal Swamp is slowly regaining its original wild character. Bears, deer, possum, other animals, and about 75 species of birds are renewing the ecological cycle evident there when George Washington first gazed on it.

Among many Dismal Swamp species is the owl, depicted by Mark Catesby of Williamsburg.

Colonial Williamsburg

8. A Dismal Swamp Portfolio

Daily Press

Washington Ditch was cut through Dismal Swamp to float timber in earlier years.

Daily Press photo by Willard Owens

Lake in Dismal Swamp was discovered by William Drummond in 1650 and named for him.

Huge cypress trees survive from ancient times in Lake Drummond at Great Dismal Swamp.

Colonial Williamsburg

Herons and other waterfowl, observed by artist Mark Catesby, live along Virginia waters.

Virginia Division of Tourism

Indians believed "Fire Bird" created Lake Drummond, perhaps a prehistoric meteor site.

Daily Press

Tidewater planters floated their tobacco to docks for shipment to Britain by convoys.

Colonial Williamsburg

9. *Tobacco Fleets to England*

THE HEADLANDS around Cape Henry and Cape Charles, along the Atlantic, were interesting places to live in colonial America for around them occurred many events of our nation's beginning.

The most important was French Admiral deGrasse's 1781 victory at the capes over a British fleet trying to reach Yorktown to rescue Cornwallis, but many other conflicts have been witnessed by the capes.

I refer chiefly to encounters between pirates and those British commercial ships which in colonial times linked Virginia with the ports of London, Bristol, Plymouth, Liverpool, Aberdeen, and Glasgow. From the early 17th century until the American Revolution, convoys of tobacco ships sailed from Hampton Roads each fall and spring, carrying hogsheads of cured orinco and sweet-scented leaf to British buyers. Virginia tobacco became a passion with British pipe smokers after it was popularized by Sir Walter Raleigh. It was the mainstay of Virginia's economy. In his book, *Tobacco Coast,* Pierce Middleton years ago detailed the operations of the Virginia and Maryland tobacco fleets. The dates of the annual departure of "the fall fleet" and "the spring fleet" were posted on courthouse, tavern, and church doors in advance so Tidewater planters could load their hogsheads—each marked with the name of the sender and of his agent in Britain—in time to be rolled aboard ship and carried to an anchorage inside the capes. There the little vessels waited the appointed date to hoist sails and follow the designated "admiral" on his British warship out into the dangerous Atlantic.

Another British warship following the convoy closely to ward off pirates and foreign attackers, was designated the "rear admiral."

A Chesapeake tobacco fleet before the Revolution might include over 200 ships. What a sight they must have made as they gathered at Lynnhaven Inlet, inside Cape Henry, at Plantation Shoals inside Cape Charles, and at other protected moorings for the three- or four-month-long voyage.

Tidewater's coast was made to order for international trade in those days of shallow-draft sailing ships. As one 18th century writer put it, "Tis the blessing of this country [Virginia] . . . and fits it extremely for the trade it carries on, that the planters can deliver their commodities at their own back doors, as the whole colony is interflowed by the most navigable rivers in the world."

Sydney King painting for Berkeley Plantation

Wealthy tobacco planters often had their own ships to sail to Britain or the Caribbean.

Added Hugh Jones, a William and Mary professor, in 1724, "No country is better watered for the conveniency of which most houses are built near some landing place; so that anything may be delivered to a gentleman there from London, Bristol, etc."

Many tobacco ships never reached Great Britain. Many sank in Atlantic storms, and others which fell behind the convoy were captured by Dutch or French privateers—fair game in the countless wars which divided Europe in those years.

And than there were pirates. From the mid-1600s till the Revolution, they periodically invaded Chesapeake Bay, often lurking near Cape Charles to attack an unescorted merchantman. The most notorious was Blackbeard, who terrorized the capes for years before he was killed in 1717 and his ship and crew seized by two British men-of-war based at Hampton.

Hampton was Virginia's chief port in the early 1700s, and British warships there kept watch over the lower Chesapeake. In fact, an early casualty of piracy in Hampton Roads, one Peter Heyman, is buried in Pembroke churchyard, near Hampton University. It was erected soon afterward by Governor Sir Francis Nicholson, who went with Heyman and British sailors aboard HMS *Shoreham* in 1700 in a successful effort to capture the French pirate Louis Guittar and his ship, *La Paix,* in Hampton Roads in 1700. Heyman's tombstone, now illegible, once read:

> In memory of Peter Heyman, Esq., grandson to Sir Peter Heyman of Summerfield in the county of Kent. He was collector of customs in the lower district of James River and went voluntarily on board the king's ship Shoreham in pursuit of a pirate who greatly infested this coast. After he had behaved himself seven hours with unlimited courage, was killed with a small shot. . . . In the engagement he stood next the Governor, upon the quarterdeck, and was here honorably interred by his order.

Once a tobacco fleet reached Great Britain and its cargo was sold by consignees, the ships were loaded up with goods ordered by planters and with other British manufactures for sale in the colonies. Most ships in colonial times returned to Virginia via the Azores or the Canary Islands, to take fresh drinking water, and thence via the Caribbean islands to Hampton Roads.

In this three-cornered trade, returning ships in the Caribbean loaded slaves, sugar, rum, and salt for transport to Virginia. Ads in Williamsburg's *Virginia Gazette* often list commodities newly received from Britain and for sale in Duke of Gloucester Street shops.

Tobacco ships were small by today's standards, often sailed by a crew of fewer than a dozen, most of them slaves. Planters had ships built in small yards on Tidewater creeks and rivers. Some vessels were owned by Scottish seaport merchants, who abounded in Norfolk, Portsmouth, Petersburg, and Alexandria. Other tobacco vessels were owned by major planters, acting individually or as partners. Among well-known owners were various Washingtons, Carters, Byrds, Harrisons, Custises, Braxtons, and Fitzhughs.

Bristol vied with London as Virginia's chief tobacco customer until 1685, when it was replaced by Glasgow. Smaller Virginia-owned ships often went only as far as the Caribbean islands, where their tobacco was reloaded on ocean vessels. In their ships, Virginians sent other products along with tobacco, corn, wheat, flour, iron, lumber, barrel staves, tar, pitch, and salted pork.

In those years the Virginia capes saw a lot of history.

Colonial Williamsburg

Tobacco was hauled to dockside in barrels and hogsheads,

Mills like this one, operated by tide, were once common in Tidewater Virginia.

Virginia Department of Argriculture

10. *Grist Mills in Tidewater*

SMALL, FAMILY-OWNED MILLS that ground corn and wheat were common in Virginia's first two centuries. The miller charged a "tithe" of 10 percent of the ground cornmeal or flour as his compensation for grinding the grain.

Remains of one of the first mills, thought to have been built by the Rev. Robert Hunt near Jamestown in 1607 or 1608, were discovered in 1937 and are recorded in the archives of the National Park Service.

It was found by accident when the Virginia Department of Transportation was building a bridge in 1937 over Powhatan Creek on Route 5, in James City County.

A news account in 1937 reports that "Highway engineers happened upon the site of Hunt's Mill, or Powhatan Mill, as it is called indiscriminately in the old records. This, they knew, must be some foreign object, as large stones are not ordinarily found in this neighborhood."

One observer was Paul Griesenauer Sr., then a Williamsburg potter. Reported the *Richmond Times-Dispatch,* "Fortunately, Griesenauer, who lives close by the bridge, was upon the scene. Knowing the rich history of this section of Powhatan Swamp . . ., he persuaded the bridge builders to dig carefully. Peeling off layer after layer of earth, the millstone was uncovered. Nearby they found sections of a wooden turbine waterwheel, further along crumbling lengths of the mill race."

Other mill remains once operated in the Williamsburg area include Coleman's Mill on Powell's Lake near Jamestown, Jones's Mill on Matoaka Lake (formerly Jones's Mill Pond) in Williamsburg; Waller Mill on Waller Pond in York County and Custis Mill on Navy land in York County.

Large millstones found at Hunt's mill included one 47 inches in diameter and 10 inches thick. The main waterwheel made of wood was excavated and found in a well-preserved state. It had been carved of one piece and was 38 inches in diameter and seven inches wide and attached to its axis with stout wooden pegs.

National Park Service research showed the equipment to be similar to that used by English and Scottish mills of the 17th century.

Griesenauer took custody of the mill equipment and sought the advice of Earl Gregg Swem, then librarian of William and Mary. The two were convinced after research that the mill was Hunt's and had been the first to be built by any

Shorn of its onetime millwheel is Causey's Mill in Newport News, once turned by current.

of Jamestown's first settlers.

The mill was built along The Maine, as Jamestown's first settlers called the narrow path they blazed to Greenspring plantation, home of several early colonial governors, and then eastward to Middle Plantation, later called Williamsburg. "The Maine" route followed high ground alongside what was once called "Powhatan's Swamp" in James City County.

The mill lay along the road designated on one early drawing of the Williamsburg area as the "Horse way over Powhatan Swamp" and also "the cart way from Middle Plantation to James Citty."

Hunt is best known in history as the founder of the Anglican (now Episcopal) church in North America and the celebrant of the first Anglican service at Jamestown in 1607. Hunt's mill was inherited by his son Thomas. In 1660 the General Assembly at Jamestown referred to "the horse way over Powhatan Swamp to James Citty at Mr. Hunt's mill," indicating that the mill still functioned.

To maintain the bridge on his land, the General Assembly gave Thomas Hunt "5,500 pounds of tobacco for repairing and maintaining the same for eight years." At the end of eight years he asked further reimbursement "for keeping the bridge open, and for mending the dam over the swamp."

Hunt's mill was later acquired by William Broadribb, who on his death in 1703 left it to his son of the same name. The younger Broadribb sold the mill to Philip Ludwell, then deputy secretary of Virginia. The Ludwell family also owned another mill on their Rich Neck plantation, adjoining Raccoon Chase and College Creek at Williamsburg. There they dammed a creek that became Jones's Millpond, now William and Mary's Lake Matoaka.

Jones's Mill continued to grind grain for York and James City farmers until World War I, according to the late Duncan Cocke, who remembered it operating in those years.

Several other such mills have recently been researched. Among known mills on the Peninsula were Young's Mill, Harwood's Mill in Warwick County, later Newport News, and Howard's Mill in Elizabeth City, later Hampton.

Colonial Williamsburg

Robertson's Windmill at Williamsburg is a re-creation of early device for grinding grain.

11. *A Ghost on the York*

WHAT WAS THE FINEST mansion in Tidewater Virginia? You could say Carters Grove, Westover, or others, but many architects think it was Rosewell in Gloucester County, now a ruin across the York River from the Yorktown Naval Weapons Station.

One of Rosewell's fans is Betty Leviner, curator of exhibition buildings for Colonial Williamsburg, who has studied countless Tidewater houses. She compares Rosewell to the Governor's Palace in Williamsburg, which set the style for luxurious Virginia living when it was built in the 1720s. But "the governor had only one cupola on his house," she said, when Mann Page had two at Rosewell.

Leviner has fascinating old photographs of Rosewell in its 19th century glory and decline. She quotes a British visitor to Virginia who wrote in 1732, "Col. Page on the North of York river is reputed [to have] the best house in Virginia."

The story of Rosewell and the Pages began at Middle Plantation, now Williamsburg, in the 1600s, when settler John Page acquired much of the acreage on which the town was later built. In 1677 Page gave the land for Bruton Parish Church, and he was James Blair's most diligent supporter in creating The College of William and Mary. The Pages in 1699 sold to the General Assembly most of the 283 acres needed to lay out the capital of Williamsburg to succeed Jamestown. After that, the family lived in Gloucester.

It was John Page's grandson, Mann Page, who began building Rosewell in the 1720s, clearly

Colonial Williamsburg

Governor John Page built Rosewell.

Colonial Williamsburg

Rosewell plantation house was fading but still habitable till early this century.

influenced by Governor Alexander Spotswood's splendid Williamsburg Palace, with its cupola and two balancing outbuildings around an impressive forecourt.

Mann Page inherited part of his wealth from his mother's family, the Manns of Gloucester, and became one of the leading Virginians of his time.

But Mann Page bit off more than he could chew. He died before he could finish his great house, leaving many debts and descendants. Foremost of the latter was John Page II, friend of Thomas Jefferson, governor of Virginia, who inherited Rosewell. Tradition has it that Jefferson, who was a schoolmate of this John Page at William and Mary, wrote some of his deathless prose in one of Rosewell's cupolas overlooking the York. It wasn't true, but it made a good story.

Bad luck dogged Rosewell. The plantation's tobacco prosperity nosedived after the American Revolution, so Mann Page's ambitious concept for his palace was never fully realized. After several generations struggled to finish it, the Pages sold it in the 1840s. Ever since then, Rosewell's fortunes have dwindled.

The new owners stripped the house of much of its elegance. Ms. Leviner described them as "either a vandal or home improver depending upon your point of view." Nevertheless, the towering house remained an imposing sight until 1916, when it burned. Even then some of its walls survived for awhile, although only frag-

After Rosewell's fire, brick walls and chimneys stood for years amid ruins.

ments survive today. Devoted friends of Rosewell are stabilizing these.

For years, Ms. Leviner tells us, "Rosewell has fascinated students—and I am definitely among that number." But virtually no family records of the house survive, many having been taken by Yankee soldiers from a Page descendant's library on Williamsburg's Palace Green during the Civil War. Descriptions of Rosewell come mostly from 19th- and 20th century sources, when the mansion's golden era was over. Experts have unearthed a few early photos that reveal the tremendous size of the structure.

Like all the dynasties that flourished in Colonial Virginia, the Pages of Rosewell and their descendants are now scattered. Like many Tidewater folk, many of the 19th-century Pages moved to Richmond or Northern Virginia when Tidewater's tobacco wealth declined. Ms. Leviner wonders why they don't have a reunion at Rosewell and see for themselves what remains of the old family seat.

There must be thousands of family members. Governor John Page alone had 12 children by one wife and eight by another.

In this century the best-known descendant was Thomas Nelson Page, novelist and romanticist, who was ambassador to Italy during the administration of Woodrow Wilson. Like many of the Pages he also descended from the Nelsons of Yorktown, whose progeny often married Page neighbors living across the York River. Genealogists have a terrible time tracing all the Page-Nelsons and the Nelson-Pages.

That's Virginia for you.

Model of HMS Charon *reveals compexity of Cornwallis' largest ship at Yorktown in 1781.*

Virginia Gazette

12. *Yorktown's Sunken Ships*

JOHN BROADWATER, archeologist with the Virginia Department of Historic Resources, has spent years diving in the York River near Yorktown's shore to recover ship artifacts. He and other archaeologists continue to preserve and identify objects brought up over the years from the muddy bottom, 20 feet below.

It's all because British General Cornwallis ordered his British station ships sunk in the York in October 1781, when he realized the American and French armies would force his surrender in the Revolution.

Broadwater's Yorktown dives ended in 1988, but he continues to take part in underwater archeology around the world as an employee of the Federal government's National Oceanic and Atmospheric Administration. He lives at Queen's Lake, near Williamsburg with his wife and two daughters.

Born in Kentucky, the scientist earned bachelor's and master's degrees and is now working on his doctorate of philosophy in underwater archaeology.

HMS *Betsy,* the British ship he excavated in the York in the 1980s, was one of nine support ships for Cornwallis' 8,000-man army at Yorktown in 1781. The 170-ton cargo vessel was ordered scuttled to keep her out of American hands. Says Broadwater, "The *Betsy* was small, little more than 75 feet long by 21 foot wide, but she was so well preserved we decided to devote all our efforts to her complete excavation rather than divide our time between all nine sunken hulls." The British had some 60 support vessels at Yorktown, Broadwater says, but most are pre-

Photo by Nan Brown

Underwater archeologist John Broadwater has dived among Yorktown's sunken ships.

sumed to have escaped before the surrender.

The largest of the nine wrecks discovered in the York is HMS *Charon* which lies on the Gloucester Point side near the Virginia Institute of Marine Science. She burned to the waterline and lies in an oyster bed that has been frequently disturbed, so Broadwater's team focused instead on a tubby little ex-coal ship which served Corn-

Virginia Gazette

A British gun from Revolutionary warship sunk at Yorktown is brought up.

wallis as a transport.

"We knew that our small ship held valuable clues to 18th-century merchant-ship life and construction," Broadwater relates. "But the York River is an archaeologist's nightmare, beset by strong and unpredictable tidal currents, near-zero visibility and persistent stinging jellyfish."

The ship and her contents lie beneath five feet of soft mud.

The problem was partly solved when the excavators devised a steel cofferdam, built around the ship, with a water purifier inside to improve underwater visibility. Using support from the National Geographic Society, the National Endowment for the Humanities, the U.S. Department of the Interior and the Commonwealth of Virginia, it took three years to design and build the dam.

To protect against stinging nettles in summer, Broadwater's divers wore wet suits, but fish were a problem. "The flounder were friendly," he reports, but "foot-long eels were more aggressive. Each time we dug a pit they would claim territorial rights, clustering around the new hole and almost pushing us aside to see what delicacies we had uncovered."

The most interesting artifacts were found in the captain's cabin. They included fancy paneling, parts of a mahogany table, an elaborate chair arm and two dozen bottles, presumably for wine or rum. Their glass had an iridescent patina caused by chemical deterioration in the York's salt water. The ship also contained "the most complete collection of barrels surviving from 18th-century America—more than three dozen in five sizes," Broadwater reveals. His divers dubbed them "Cornwallis' hot tubs."

Buried in the ballast of the ship's hold were three barrels packed with 10,000 lead musket balls. Other barrels held wine, rum and water. From her contents, Broadwater concludes that the *Charon* was a floating workshop for Cornwallis' forces. "We found scores of partly trimmed logs, beams and plans. . . . All these were indications that a variety of items were being fabricated for other ships or land fortifica-

Daily Press

Wine bottles from Cornwalli's sunken ships are lifted from York at Yorktown.

tions." The archaeologist estimates she was a 170-ton vessel, probably built as a coal carrier on England's east coast.

When Cornwallis marched his army up the Atlantic Coast from South Carolina in the spring of 1781 and decided to make a stand at Yorktown, supporting British transports and supply ships steamed into the York. British ships then controlled the river upland to West Point, and timber and other supplies were collected from within that area.

Broadwater's research indicates that the British ship carried "a small crew—just the captain, the first mate, and a handful of seamen. The most experienced sailors would handle the tasks of carpenter and bosun."

Broadwater's diving followed strict safety and

scientific procedures. "Suction dredges vacuumed up blanketing silt," Broadwater reports, "which was strained for small items before being expelled over the side. The muck that hindered excavation had preserved organic materials, from corncobs to 10-foot logs. Hundreds of feet of rope in various sizes were found."

Broadwater's investigations are the latest in the Yorktown-Gloucester point area since 1781. The first were made by French forces, which were permitted by George Washington to recover British cargo and ships after Cornwallis' surrender. Then, in 1934–35, Peninsula divers located the remains of nine ships, in a project sponsored by the Mariners' Museum, Newport News Shipbuilding and National Park Service. Many wine bottles and other artifacts from that project are exhibited at the Mariners' Museum and at the Park Service's Yorktown Visitor Center.

Revolutionary Yorktown and the long-continued underwater archaeological research of Cornwallis' British ships are the subject of an interesting account Broadwater wrote for *National Geographic Magazine.*

13. *Building New Point Light*

MATHEWS is one of those off-the-beaten-track counties, yet its fringed shoreline on Chesapeake Bay, Mobjack Bay and the Piankatank River is one of the most picturesque in America, as countless retirees have discovered in recent years.

Once Mathews was home to farmers and fishermen, but those livelihoods have declined since World War II. Now its farms and dockside houses are being gobbled up by come-heres, fleeing the trauma of city life: heavy traffic, high taxes and threats to life and property. Its development has also been hastened by the Coleman Bridge, linking Yorktown and Gloucester.

If Mathews has a trademark, it's the old New Point Comfort Lighthouse that stands serenely at the juncture of Mobjack and Chesapeake bays. Although the lighthouse no longer is maintained by the Coast Guard as a navigational aid, the prim old lady is being preserved by an $80,000 fund raised by volunteers after Mathews County took over the property from Uncle Sam in 1976.

Virginians no longer make much of their living on the water, but in Colonial times New Point Comfort at the tip of the Middle Peninsula was an important landmark for Chesapeake mariners. "New Point" appeared in Virginia records in 1641, linked with the earlier Old Point Comfort in Hampton.

The present lighthouse was built in 1801, costing the federal government of President Thomas Jefferson only $8,750 for two acres of land plus the sandstone beacon (63 feet tall) and a keeper's house. The latter was razed in 1919 after the lighthouse was mechanized.

But the furies of wind, rain and sun continue to threaten the 1801 lighthouse. Storms severed New Point Comfort from the mainland in 1847, although waders once could reach the light at low tide. More recently, the tower's decay has necessitated a grant from the Virginia Department of Conservation and Historic Resources. Now perilously poised on a narrow, seagirt land spit, the tower can no longer be reached by land. However, its nearby coves remain popular with picnickers and pleasure boatsmen.

From its beginning, Mathews has enjoyed its remoteness. It was a parish of Gloucester County until 1790, when it became a separate county. Its early watermen were ministered to in the 19th century by Isaiah Thomas, an itinerant Methodist who came by boat from Maryland's Eastern Shore, ministering to Chesapeake's fishing people.

New Point on Chesapeake Bay is no longer active lighthouse but a Mathews historic site.

Today Mathews is notable, with the rest of the Middle Peninsula and Northern Neck, for its many white clapboard Methodist and Baptist churches, built in the heyday of Protestant evangelism, before World War II. They have charm, however simply or homemade. New Point was a favored site of church picnics back when all-day boating parties were popular, before automobiles. Writes Benjamin Trask in the *Mariners' Museum Journal.*

> Church social goers and vacationers from as far away as Hampton Roads made the trip to the point to enjoy the salty air and admire the attractive lighthouse. A 1902 pilot's manual claimed that boats 'come to anchor for the night inside the New Point Comfort Lighthouse,' in the draft of 12 to 21 feet of water.

After New Point Light's deactivation, the Coast Guard replaced it with a smaller signal light, about 1,000 yards away. It flashes a light and sounds a horn blast every 20 seconds from September 15 to June 1.

Not far from New Point on the Chesapeake is Wolftrap Light, named for an English ship, the *Wolf,* which went aground there in the mid-17th century. It created a celebrated early Virginia lawsuit. The unmarked shoal remained a threat to mariners until a light was installed there in the 18th century to assist vessels traversing Mathews' Chesapeake Bay waterfront.

When I visit Gloucester Point each summer, I like to drive around the Gloucester-Mathews countryside, admiring the farms, churches and the thriving vegetable and flower gardens. I note that many churchyards have above-ground burials because the land is barely above water-level.

The best way to appreciate the picturesque mixture of land, creeks, beaches and bay is by flying over it, in a plane.

Although Route 17 through Gloucester County is being urbanized, the more remote Mathews

County has escaped much development. Most newcomers, I'm told, want to own a tract of several acres in order to insure privacy. Thus far, most of Mathews' development has been fairly upscale. Apparently the 60- or 70-mile distance to Newport News has discouraged most Peninsula commuters.

And what of the future? The greenhouse effect is said to be warming the earth's temperature, slowly thawing more of the polar ice caps and slowly raising the earth's sea levels. A half-century hence, the Atlantic coastal water level might be five feet higher than today's, which would inundate a lot of Virginia's coastal periphery. Mathews and Gloucester would be severely affected if that scenario comes true.

But we moderns have enough present worries without anticipating that one. As for me, I plan to keep coming to Gloucester and driving through the Middle Peninsula's byways.

God doesn't make places like Mathews and Gloucester any more.

Virginia Division of Tourism

Pound net fishing, shown at Tangier, was once common but now declining for lack of fish.

14. *Conflict on the York*

THE YORK RIVER figured prominently in the American Revolution and also was the scene of a minor battle in the War of 1812: a fight between the tiny U.S. revenue cutter *Surveyor* and a British frigate, HMS *Narcissus.*

The fight took place June 12, 1813, off Gloucester Point and it was a prelude to the much bigger British naval attack on Craney Island near Norfolk on June 19. After the British were repelled there by the Virginia militia, they vengefully invaded and laid waste to Hampton on June 25.

All this action preceded the British sacking of Washington, D.C., in the spring of 1814. Then they burned the White House and sent President James Madison fleeing into the hinterland.

As the *Surveyor* was the ancestor of today's Coast Guard cutters, the service takes a bit of justified pride in her heroism. The incident is summed up in a Coast Guard history:

> The Cutter *Surveyor,* of six 12-pound carronades, was lying in York River under the command of Mr. Samuel Travis. Her crew consisted of 15 men. At nightfall she was attacked by the boats of the British frigate *Narcissus,* containing about 50 men, under the command of Lt. John Crerie.
>
> The crew waited until the British were within pistol shot before they opened their fire; the latter dashed gallantly on, however, and at once carried [captured] the cutter. But though brief, the struggle was bloody: five of the crew were wounded, and of the British, three men were killed and seven wounded. Lt. Crerie [British commander] considered his opponents to have shown so much bravery that he returned to Mr. Travis his sword, with a letter as complimentary to him as it was creditable to the writer.

Travis and his crew were carried off and their cutter was impounded by the British.

Those were the days of genteel warfare. The British victor's letter to Travis is part of the Coast Guard's proud history. It reads simply:

> Sir: Your gallant and desperate attempt to defend your vessel against more than double your number . . . excited such admiration . . . as I have seldom witnessed, and induced me to return you the sword you had so ably used. Our poor fellows have severely suffered, occasioned chiefly if not solely by the precaution you had taken to prevent surprise. I am at a loss which to admire most, the previous arrangement on board the *Surveyor* or the determined manner in which the deck

Glimpses of Tidewater Life 49

Schooners were workhorse vessels in 19th century Virginia waters, like this three master.

was disputed, inch by inch.

You have my most sincere wishes for the immediate parole and speedy exchange of yourself and brave crew and cannot but regret that I myself have no influence that way.

Otherwise it would be forthcoming. I am sir, with much respect, your most obedient servant, John Crerie.

Apparently, the *Surveyor* was encountered by the British while they were reconnoitering the Tidewater area. The British ships, under admirals Sir John Warren and George Cockburn, had entered the Capes on February 4, 1813, and blockaded United States shipping.

Soon Virginia militiamen encamped around Hampton Roads, fearing attack. Governor John Barbour came from Richmond to confer with Brigadier General Robert Barraud Taylor, a Norfolk lawyer who commanded the 10,000 Virginia militia defenders.

The British finally decided to invade desolate Craney Island, near Norfolk. Using shallow-draft barges, they landed nearly 2,500 infantrymen and marines. However, the Virginians' heavy fire drove them back to their ships.

The *Norfolk Gazette and Public Ledger* reported next day that "The enemy has been

Colonial Williamsburg

1813 York River battle between British and American ships was at Gloucester Point, right.

completely foiled in an enterprise of great importance and without the loss of one man on our part, or even one wounded...."

But the British sought revenge. On the night of June 24 they landed again, this time, as the *Norfolk Gazette* reported, "at New-Port-Neuse, at the entrance of James River." By sunup, the landing force had reached Celey's, the Cary plantation bordering Hampton Roads on today's Chesapeake Avenue.

Evading most of the Virginia defenders, the British marched to Hampton and laid waste to the town of 1,000 people. Even a British officer, Colonel Charles Napier, wrote that "Every horror was perpetrated with impunity—rape, murder, pillage and not a man was punished." He blamed it chiefly on French troops that had been hired by the British.

Americans were deeply angered, but young America lacked the naval power to defend itself. The British returned next spring and sacked Washington, D.C. Tiny Virginia vessels like *Surveyor* were no defense against men-of-war.

When the War of 1812 ended, President Monroe insisted that the nation build coastal forts for defense. The largest, named for Monroe himself and situated at Old Point, stands as a reminder of the British invasion of Hampton Roads in 1813.

Maryland Historical Society

Tiny U.S. revenue cutter Surveyor, *similar to vessels above, fought bravely in 1813.*

Admiral Sir George Cookburn was blamed for burning Hampton in War of 1812.

Virginia State Library

15. *When the British Burned Hampton*

THE ASSAULT by the British on Hampton in 1813 destroyed much of that town, but it strengthened the nation's will to build Fort Monroe and avert future attacks. The so-called "Burning of Hampton" (it was more a pillaging) killed a few people and removed a lot of property, but it was far less destructive than the town's self-inflicted second burning during the Civil War when only St. John's Church was left standing.

After gutting Hampton, the Redcoats went on to burn Havre de Grace, Maryland, and the Capitol in Washington. The useless war ended in a draw. Neither side won.

In the spring of 1813, Virginia sent 10,000 militiamen under Brigadier General Robert Barraud Taylor of Norfolk to defend both sides of Hampton Roads. Great Britain's invasion began in June when 20 British naval ships entered Hampton Roads.

At Craney Island, the British were turned back. One of the participants of this action, James Jarvis, a 22-year-old sergeant in the Portsmouth Rifles, wrote, in 1846, an account of the battle. Shortly after the engagement, Jarvis quit the militia and operated a boat-building yard at Portsmouth. He later inspected timbers for Gosport Navy Yard, now the Norfolk Naval Shipyard. Jarvis' recollections are now in Swem Library at The College of William and Mary.

The British raid on Norfolk was aborted and the British waited a day or two before launching a pre-dawn strike of landing barges at Hampton Creek. Then, while some Virginians were preoccupied there, other British troop barges landed near Celey's plantation on the present Boulevard and Redcoats marched at dawn to Hampton. The British force numbered 2,500. The British command was under Admiral Sir John Warren, commander-in-chief of British naval forces in America, whose underlings were George Cockburn and General Sir Sydney Beckwith. Cockburn's duty was to get British troops ashore where Beckwith would lead them against the Virginians.

Commanding Hampton's militia defenders was Major Stapleton Crutchfield. In a letter to Governor James Barbour on June 28, 1813, Crutchfield described the action. He reported that the British lost 200 soldiers at Hampton, while the Virginians lost about 20. What infuriated Virginia and the nation was the conduct of the British forces. Crutchfield protested to the governor:

The unfortunate females of Hampton who could not leave the town were suffered to be

51

52   *Along Virginia's Golden Shores*

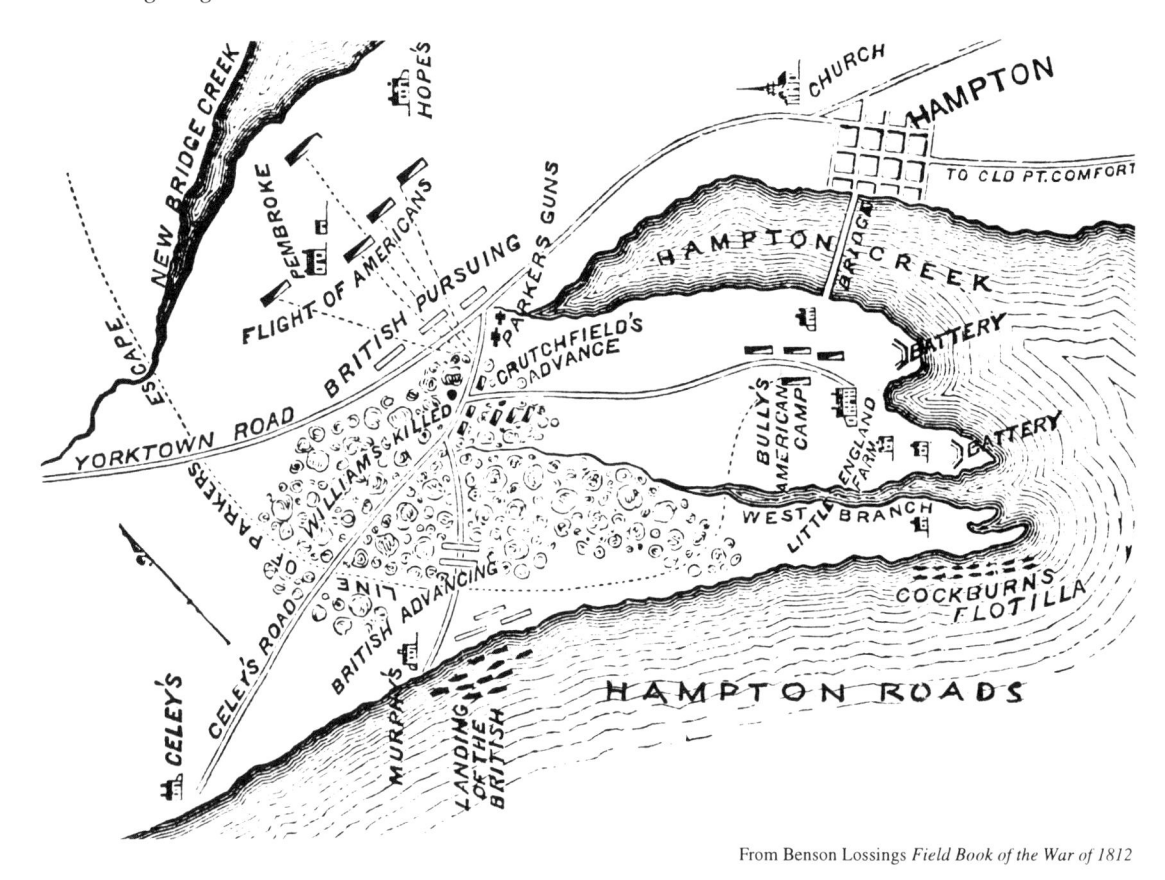

Early map of Hampton shows British strategy in 1813 burning of little town.

From Benson Lossings *Field Book of the War of 1812*

abused in the most shameful manner, not only by the venal savage foe but by the unfortunate and infuriated blacks. They pillaged and encouraged every act of raping, murder, killing a poor man by the name of Kirby, who had been lying on point of death for more than six months, shooting his wife . . . and killing his faithful dog.

Another Virginian, thought to be Colonel Richard E. Parker of Westmoreland County, protested to the *Richmond Enquirer* that the British violated rules of civilized warfare. He reported:

> The town and country adjacent was given up to indiscriminate plunder of a licentiate soldiery. . . . Every article of valuable property was taken. . . . In many cases not even a knife or fork or plate was left. . . . The church was pillaged, and the silverplate belonging to it was taken away, although inscribed with the donor's name. The windmills in the neighborhood were stripped of their sails.

Parker observed that the loot was taken to the shoreside headquarters of Cockburn and Beckwith. "Hampton exhibits a dreary and desolate appearance which no American can witness unmoved," Parker wrote. Taylor strongly protested to Warren. Warren, quartered aboard his Britannic Majesty's flagship, *San Domingo*, anchored in Hampton Roads, asked Beckwith to reply for him. Promptly, Beckwith wrote Parker that the British were retaliating for Virginians' callous shooting of defenseless British soldiers clinging to their sunken barge at Craney Island a few days earlier.

Taylor then sent his aide, Captain John Myers (whose Myers house still stands in Norfolk) to

Old Point Comfort to dispatch a report of British offenses to Secretary of War John Armstrong in Washington. Myers talked with Beckwith, who admitted that his invaders had inflicted unauthorized damages on Hampton, but he blamed it on mercenary French troops, the Chasseurs Britanniques.

Taylor wrote Armstrong: "There is too much reason to believe that before the attack on Craney Island, the cupidity of the troops had been excited by a promise of the pillage of Norfolk."

Apologizing for French excesses, the British sailed out of Hampton Roads on to new offenses in Havre de Grace and Washington.

Meantime, "Remember Hampton!" became a battle cry. That's why President James Monroe in 1819 proposed building America's largest coastal fort at Old Point.

Craney Island is sandy obstruction in Hampton Roads at entrance to Norfolk's harbor.

*General Simon
Bernard of France
designed Fort Monroe.*

Casemate Museum

16. *Fortifying Hampton Roads*

SOME OF THE MOST EXPENSIVE real estate in Hampton Roads languishes unused today. It's the Rip Raps, a man-made island of a half-dozen acres adjoining the Hampton Roads Bridge-Tunnel which once served as the site of the summer White House.

It was built at great cost with material dredged

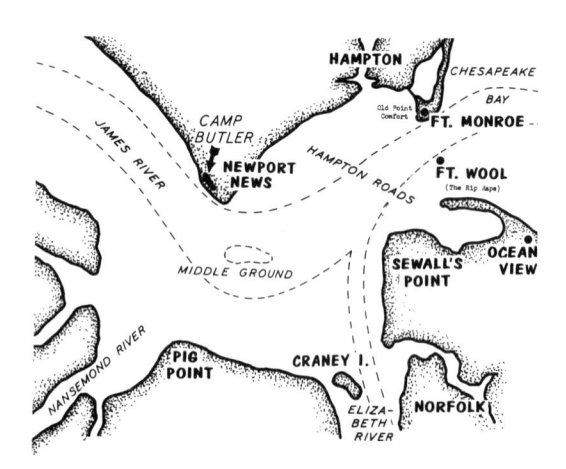

Chester Bradley

Fort Monroe dominated channel from Chesapeake Bay into Hampton Roads and its cities.

up in the 1830s and '40s when Fort Monroe was being built at Old Point Comfort. Its only wartime use came during the Civil War when the Army and Navy placed guns there to help control the harbor.

How did the ugly little sandspit come into existence in the first place?

It was designed to control the eastern side of the mile-wide Hampton Roads channel between Old Point Comfort and Willoughby Spit.

In 1813, the British navy sailed into Hampton Roads unchallenged and laid waste to Craney Island and Hampton. After James Monroe became president in 1816, he and his secretary of war, John C. Calhoun, to avert a recurrence, proposed building a dozen coastal forts from New England to the Gulf Coast, at the nation's principal harbors. Fort Monroe was the largest and is the only one still in active service.

Originally called Fort Calhoun or Castle Calhoun, the Rip Raps was to be linked in wartime to Fort Monroe by a "log-boom" of floating planks connected by chains. And, indeed, during World War I and II an anti-submarine net was set out by the Navy in that area.

The sandspit proved far costlier to build in the 1830s and 1840s than the Army estimated.

54

Old Point Comfort was fortified in 1820s as Fort Monroe to protect from sea invasion.

Dredged mud kept sliding into the water despite the "rip raps," or broken rocks installed to contain it. When Lafayette returned from France to tour Revolutionary sites in Virginia in 1824, he visited Fort Calhoun.

From 1831 to 1834, Lieutenant Robert E. Lee of the United States Corps of Engineers was stationed at Fort Monroe and supervised construction of the island fort. Surprisingly, the Rip Raps appealed to two United States presidents as a vacation retreat.

Andrew Jackson stayed there several weeks in the summers of 1831, 1833 and 1835. In July 1833, the *Norfolk Herald* reported that President Jackson's "Hotel at the Rip Raps is a delightful summer residence." Jackson declined a visit to Norfolk that August in order "to remain free from bustle and fatigue."

John Tyler stayed there in 1842 after the death of his first wife, Letitia Christian Tyler. The quarters on the Rip Raps where Presidents Jackson and Tyler had lived burned in 1846 and were not replaced.

In 1862, the Army renamed Fort Calhoun as Fort Wool in honor of General John Wool, a Mexican War hero who commanded Fort Monroe.

When President Abraham Lincoln came to Fort Monroe on May 8, 1862, a few days after General George B. McClellan and his huge Army of the Potomac had captured Williamsburg at the start of the Peninsula campaign, he inspected new coast artillery guns erected on the Rip Raps. The next day Lincoln returned to Fort Wool to observe the bombardment of the Confederates across the water at Sewells Point. That attack preceded the Union's capture of Norfolk and the Norfolk Navy Yard at Portsmouth.

For a brief time during the Civil War, Fort Wool was used as a prison. The commanding general of Fort Monroe stopped that use in 1862, saying, "The water is bad and the heat is intense, and no citizen should be sent there for a light cause and without pretty clear evidence of guilt."

In 1902, the Army built five concrete coastal artillery batteries on Fort Wool, and during World War I they were fully manned. Personnel stationed on the Rip Raps also tended the antisubmarine net that stretched to Fort Monroe.

Fort Wool lay unused for 20 years, until the outbreak of World War II when it was re-armed

56 *Along Virginia's Golden Shores*

with anti-aircraft guns, and an anti-submarine net was again installed.

British actor Alec Guinness, who commanded a British vessel which entered Hampton Roads in the 1940s, ran his ship afoul of the net—an incident he later recorded in his autobiography.

The Rips Raps was given to Virginia in 1967 by the United States government, and later ownership was transferred to the city of Hampton. Summer sightseers can take a cruise boat from Hampton to visit it.

Daily Press

First Chamberlin Hotel and Government Pier once crowned Fort Monroe's Waterfront.

Chesapeake naval explosion changed life of John Tyler.

17. *John Tyler's Virginia*

FEBRUARY 28, 1844, should have been a great day for the navy. The first propeller-driven steam warship, USS *Princeton*, was to christen two of her revolutionary new 12-inch guns, specially designed and cast by skilled gunsmiths.

On board when the warship sailed from Washington D.C., to cruise down the Potomac River were President John Tyler and about 250 VIPS. The widowed Dolley Madison was among them, along with Secretary of State Abel P. Upshur and Secretary of the Navy Thomas Walker Gilmer, both Virginians. The others were senators and congressmen and Navy officials, all warmly dressed for the cruise to Mount Vernon and return.

But what started as a gala outing ended in tragedy.

Tyler had become president on April 4, 1841, on the death in the White House of President William Henry Harrison. He had to be summoned by a messenger, who arrived at Tyler's house on Francis Street in Williamsburg at dawn and rushed him back to Washington to be sworn in. Tyler was the first vice president to succeed a president in office.

But in time Tyler became bitterly unpopular with fellow Whigs. They called him "the president by mistake" and "a president without a party." That was after he defied Whig sentiment to veto a bill creating a national bank. He'd been drafted by the Whigs as vice president to give Southern strength to their ticket, overlooking the fact that he opposed the bank and other Whig measures.

But the 1844 Potomac outing was a non-partisan celebration. Wrote Tyler, "Never did the eye gaze on a brighter or more animated scene than that which the beautiful river exhibited. The decks were soon crowded with happy visitors."

Once the *Princeton* reached the firing area, her new guns were fired four times. Then, on the fifth firing, something went wrong. The 50-pound powder charge created so great an explosion that it split one wrought-iron gun barrel and showered those on deck with burning powder and shrapnel.

Wrote one guest, "The scene upon the deck may more easily be imagined than described. Nor can the imagination picture itself half of the horrors."

Bodies were crashed by shrapnel, which struck all who stood near the guns. Dead were Secretaries Upshur and Gilmer, plus two dozen

Virginia Gazette

President Tyler once lived in Williamsburg at Francis and South England Streets.

others, many of them federal officials.

One survivor shrieked, "The Secretary of State is dead," but there were many others dead and dying. Among those killed was Senator David Gardiner of New York, whose beautiful 23-year-old daughter, Julia, was overwhelmed with grief.

President Tyler sought to console Julia Gardiner and prevent her seeing her father's mangled corpse. "My dear child, you can do no good," he urged. "Your father is in heaven." When Julia fainted, she awakened in the president's arms. At Alexandria she had to be carried off the ship.

Tyler's concern for Julia Gardiner grew into love, and the widowed president married her four months later in the White House. When his term ended in 1845—the Whigs didn't offer to renominate him —he bought a Charles City County farmhouse, naming it Sherwood Forest and likening himself to the outlawed Robin Hood. There they lived until his death in 1862. One of his sons by Julia was Lyon Gardiner Tyler, a lawyer and historian, who became president of The College of William and Mary in 1888.

The Princeton gun explosion was only one of many difficulties which befell Tyler in his four years in office. Most arose from the fact that he was essentially a states' rights and slave-owning Democrat, at odds with the Whigs who had elected him. Thus, when they tried to set up the Bank of the United States, Tyler promptly vetoed it. Immediately, every member of his cabinet resigned except Daniel Webster, secretary of state, who had succeeded Abel Upshur.

A man of strong opinion and no compromise, Tyler had earlier resigned from the Senate rather than follow the instructions of the Virginia General Assembly to vote for a motion to expunge Senator Henry Clay's censure of Andrew Jackson from Senate records. Many years later, John F. Kennedy cited Tyler for political integrity in his book, *Profiles in Courage*.

The house wherein Tyler resided in Williamsburg with his first wife and family stood at the juncture of Francis and South England Streets. Part of the site is now used for parking by the adjacent Williamsburg Lodge. Surviving in Charles City County are Tyler's Sherwood Forest, now open to visitors, and his birthplace nearby, called Greenway.

II

The Age of Steam

Cecil Page

Gloucester native Thomas Jefferson Page commanded first Confederate battery on the York.

18. *Civil War's First Shots*

IN THE SPRING OF 1861 life changed greatly in Tidewater. Virginia became an armed camp. The Peninsula was a natural invasion route for Union troops from Fort Monroe to move toward the Confederate stronghold of Richmond.

Against this background, historian Peter Wrike has examined the events of those dawning months of the Civil War on the Gloucester-Mathews peninsula.

The Yankees didn't come immediately. During most of April and May, 1861, both sides held back until, on May 23—inflamed by President Lincoln's call to the state to put down the rebellion that began with the firing on Fort Sumter, South Carolina, on April 15—Virginians voted to secede.

In Gloucester County, the 21st Regiment of the Virginia Militia was called to active service. Since Colonial times, such county units had met periodically to train to defend the community in case of need. "Gloucester Point was fortified," Wrike writes, "and artillery from Richmond was stationed there." At first only three small cannon were available to discourage Yankee ships from coming up the York River. When a United States Navy reconnaissance ship, the *Yankee,* came up the York from Fort Monroe, the little battery got its first baptism of fire.

"The *Yankee* turned and steamed rapidly back to Fort Monroe," Wrike writes. These shots were the first of the Civil War in Virginia.

A Gloucester native, Thomas Jefferson Page, who had resigned his United States Navy commission, at first commanded the Gloucester Point battery. He was one of several Gloucester men who served the Confederacy illustriously, including General William Booth Taliaferro and General Henry Lane.

When secession came, Gloucester's 21st Regiment mobilized for action. Its members—most of them 18 to 35—gave up fishing or farming to train in camps at Gloucester Point and elsewhere, awaiting the Peninsula Campaign that finally developed under General George McClellan in 1862.

Once at war, Gloucester's 21st "raised additional companies of infantry," Wrike writes. "These and others were stationed at Gloucester Point and Yorktown. For almost a year they remained close to home. When sick, they usually went home or to Gloucester houses serving as hospitals."

Wholesale warfare enveloped the Peninsula

in the spring of 1862, after the Confederate ship *Virginia* had battled the USS *Monitor* in Hampton Roads off Newport News and after Union forces had captured Norfolk. On the Peninsula, General John B. Magruder—the swashbuckler called "Prince John"—initially commanded Confederate forces at Yorktown, Williamsburg, Hampton and Newport News. He and his troops built dams and revetments to hold back McClellan's onslaught. After Federal invasion loomed, the Confederacy sent General Joseph E. Johnston down to defend the Peninsula, replacing Magruder.

After McClellan captured Yorktown and led his army west to Williamsburg in April and May, 1862, Virginia disbanded its home-based militia and inducted its men into full service. Boys who had never been outside Gloucester were sent to distant posts.

Writes Wrike: "They knew Gloucester would be undefended with the retreat of Confederate forces. Their homes, families, friends would not be protected from invasion."

Despite such concerns, nearly all Gloucester men in the 21st Militia went on to enlist in the Confederate units.

A Gloucester mother, Mary Hunley, wrote: "My two sons have left to join the regiment.... It was heart-breaking to part from two such sons. None but a mother can have an idea of the anguish that filled my soul."

After Gloucester's young men marched away, boys under 18 and elderly men formed a home guard. But they were no match for the trained Federal troops that from 1862 to 1865 held Yorktown, Gloucester Point and the York River.

Typical of Gloucester soldiers was Joseph J. Robins, who enlisted in 1863 at 18 in the 5th Virginia Cavalry. He was killed six months later at Spotsylvania. In the same unit, Major John Puller of Gloucester was killed at Kelly's Fort near Fredericksburg, fighting under Jeb Stuart.

After the Federals seized Yorktown and Gloucester Point in 1862, they kept the Gloucester countryside terrified by periodic raids. Wrote Mary Hunley: "I am told the Yankees are coming in the night. God only knows what will be our fate."

After the war, Union Admiral Samuel DuPont, whose U.S. naval forces had controlled the York during the war, wrote that "A large amount of property was destroyed in these raids. It was impossible to discriminate, and, in consequence, a great many innocent people suffered." It took them a long time to forgive the Yankees.

Although it escaped the worst ravages the Peninsula suffered, Gloucester was impoverished by the war and suffered well into this century.

In memory of its defenders, the county erected a Confederate monument at Gloucester Courthouse in 1889, and it stands there today to recall the saddest of all America's wars.

Many Gloucester men enlisted in Confederate service at the courthouse in 1861.

Southerner David Farragut stuck with Union navy, became hero.

19. Burning the Navy Yard

THE MOST IMPORTANT Virginia shipyard before the Newport News yard was started by Collis Huntington in 1886 was the Norfolk Navy Yard in Portsmouth on the Elizabeth River. The "Norfolk" was to avert confusion with another Navy shipyard at Portsmouth, New Hampshire. Today the yard in Portsmouth is largely a ship-repair operation, for the Navy long ago found private yards do better work at lower cost than government ones.

When Virginia seceded in April 1861, President Abraham Lincoln's war cabinet was concerned about the future of the Portsmouth yard and other federal installations in Virginia. Would the yard and Fort Monroe stick with the Union or be seized by Confederates?

The Portsmouth yard meant a lot to the Union. Berthed or drydocked there when Virginia seceded were the *Pennsylvania,* the Navy's largest ship, as well as two other major warships, three frigates, two sloops of war, and smaller vessels. Most important, Portsmouth harbored the 275-foot steam frigate *Merrimack,* which was under repair.

The yard's commandant was Captain Charles McCauley, an indecisive man whose sympathies were dangerously uncertain. Accordingly, when Virginia seceded, the Navy ordered the *Merrimack* to leave for the "safer" port of Philadelphia. Union fears were soon confirmed when Confederates seized three U.S. lightships at Norfolk and sank them in the channel off Sewell's Point. The war was on.

Commandant McCauley was clearly torn by his conflicting loyalty to the Unites States Navy and to his fellow workers and Portsmouth residents, mostly Confederates. As Donald Shomette was to write, "It would be a race between the Union and the Confederacy, with the Norfolk Navy Yard and all that lay within it as first prize. . . . The first mission [of the Virginia Navy] was to wrest control of the Navy Yard from the North."

While the yard seethed with bitterness between Unionists and Confederates, two companies of Virginia Navy volunteers plus militiamen of the Norfolk Grays mustered outside the yard, hoping to force McCauley into thinking he was surrounded by Confederate guns. They almost succeeded.

McCauley finally decided his best course was to blow up the Navy yard and all its ships to avert Confederate seizure. He was unaware that

63

Federals tried to destroy Portsmouth's Navy yard to prevent its falling to Confederates.

the USS *Pawnee* was en route at that very moment down the Potomac River from Washington with a strong force United States Marines to help hold the shipyard. But it arrived too late.

Old Navy hands hated to see warships scuttled. Guns aboard ships were spiked, and ammunition was thrown overboard. When the *Pawnee* arrived, the once-proud shipyard was a shambles. McCauley's men had put out of use 2,000 naval guns, 300 of them of the latest pattern, plus other armament.

The Navy then decided to blow up the yard's dry dock, built in Revolutionary times and one of the nation's biggest. This was to keep it out of Confederate use. After that, all naval personnel adhering to the Union set fire to the yard and sailed for Washington.

Writes Donald Shomette, "The view of the Norfolk Naval Yard ablaze in the night was to the loyal Union men a sight of unforgettable grandeur and sadness. The Navy's most important yard on the mid-Atlantic seaboard had been destroyed along with an enormously powerful segment of the Union navy itself."

The navy's abandonment of the yard left the Confederacy happily in possession of 1,200 heavy guns, 2,800 barrels of powder, machinery and other useful armament. The USS *Merrimack* was raised by the Confederates to be converted into the CSS *Virginia* and to fight the USS *Monitor* in Hampton Roads the next year. Other Union warships were also raised.

But the Union eventually got revenge. Later in the war its forces retook the Norfolk Navy Yard and rebuilt it. President Lincoln came down from Washington and observed the victory with satisfaction. By that time what little navy the Confederacy ever had was overawed by the Union's.

Throughout the war, Union warships blockaded the James and York rivers, and only a few daring Confederate blockade runners eluded them. The Union Navy largely succeeded in blockading the Confederacy's coast, from the Atlantic off the Eastern Shore southward around the Gulf of Mexico. That cut off Southern shipments of cotton and tobacco to Europe and denied the South munitions it needed from neutral nations.

One Union naval hero in all this was Admiral David Farragut, a Southerner but a Unionist, who moved from Norfolk to New York when Virginia seceded. He eventually led Federal gunboats up the Mississippi River and forced New Orleans to surrender. He was called "the outstanding naval figure of the war" and was the first man to become a vice admiral and full admiral in the U.S. Navy.

Portsmouth's Navy Yard has long since been rebuilt, and evidence of its Civil War crises obliterated. But not forgotten.

General George B. McClellan led 125,000 Union troops on Peninsula but failed at Richmond.

20. *War on the Peninsula*

CAN YOU IMAGINE what George Bush would have done in the war with Iraq if General Norman Schwarzkopf had peppered him from the battlefront with complaints that the president was dooming his soldiers to military defeat?

Well, complain was what General George McClellan did in 1862 while he was on the Peninsula moving slowly westward to Richmond in the Civil War's first major campaign to crush the Confederate "rebellion."

In Washington, exasperated President Lincoln sent repeated dispatches to his field commander urging him to attack the enemy aggressively. They did no good.

The Lincoln-McClellan exchange was aired by McClellan in a book he published in 1864 as campaign literature when he ran for president on the Democratic ticket against Lincoln. Though handily defeated, McClellan stayed in public life and was governor of New Jersey from 1878 to 1881. He was an able man in most respects.

McClellan's problem was excessive caution. Although Lincoln had given him a huge 125,000-man army, McClellan believed Robert E. Lee had 200,000 soldiers defending Richmond. Actually, Lee had only 65,000 at most.

In his attempted self-defense, McClellan reprinted endless telegrams and letters that flowed from the Peninsula in 1862 between him and his Washington superiors—Lincoln and War Secretary Edwin M. Stanton. McClellan had led his army down the Potomac from Washington to Fort Monroe in April 1862, a year after Virginia seceded. In a week, he had moved his army close to Yorktown, where he faced Confederate General Joseph E. Johnston's Confederates who were entrenched behind Yorktown's Revolutionary defenses, dug for the siege by Cornwallis 81 years earlier, in 1781.

McClellan wrote in an optimistic tone to his superiors when he started into Virginia, but at Yorktown he began to worry about losing. He wrote Secretary Stanton from there on April 7: "Since my arrangements were made for this campaign, at least 50,000 men have been taken from my command."

When McClellan delayed in attacking, Lincoln told him on April 9, "Your dispatches, complaining that you are not properly sustained, while they do no offend me, do pain me very much." Lincoln concluded, "I have never written you, or spoken yo you, in greater kindness of feeling than now. . . . But you must act."

After its Confederate defenders burned Hampton, Union moved in for Peninsula Campaign.

After the Confederate defenders retreated from Yorktown to Fort Magruder, east of Williamsburg, McClellan finally attacked Johnston's 20,000 troops on May 5 and forced them to abandon Williamsburg and flee westward through the Chickahominy swamps. McClellan stayed behind several days in Williamsburg's Palmer House (then called the Vest house), writing complaints to Lincoln and Stanton.

"Little Mac" clearly was alarmed at the prospect of attacking Richmond. Writing to Stanton on May 10 from camp at Benjamin Ewell's farm, four miles west of Williamsburg, he whined that "If I am not reinforced, it is probable that I will be obliged to fight nearly double my numbers." Actually, the advantage was his.

The huge Yankee army floundered for weeks as spring rains fell on Charles City and New Kent. When Lincoln withheld promised Federal troops (Abe wanted to defend the District of Columbia against Confederate attack), McClellan protested violently. Fed up, Lincoln wrote McClellan on May 25, "I think the time is near when you must either attack Richmond or give up the job and come back to the defense of Washington. Let me hear from you instantly."

McClellan replied he was about to strike.

After the Confederate commander Joseph E. Johnston was injured in June in the battle at Fair Oaks, outside Richmond, President Jefferson Davis chose Robert E. Lee to protect Richmond. The ensuing "Seven Days' Battles" east of Richmond were hotly fought. Casualties were so heavy on both sides that Richmond's tobacco warehouses were filled with unburied dead.

In the heat of that campaign, McClellan wrote to Secretary Stanton, "If I save this army now, I tell you plainly that I owe no thanks to you, or to any other persons in Washington."

Alarmed at the prospect of being enveloped by Lee's imagined hordes, McClellan finally turned back down the Peninsula and led his weary army into rest camp at Berkeley Plantation, where they enjoyed the protection of Navy ships in the James River at Harrison's Landing.

There Lincoln met with McClellan and called off the Peninsula Campaign.

A few months later, in November 1862, Lincoln removed the general from command of the Army of the Potomac.

Even so, McClellan remained popular with his enlisted men of his army and with his Democratic party, which chose him in 1864 to run against Lincoln for the presidency. Abe easily won, and the following year won the war.

Daily Press

After Confederates burned Hampton, former slaves built "Slabtown" houses and moved in.

21. *The Lee Family of Lee Hall*

AT THE TIME of the Civil War, the Peninsula had few residents except those who lived in the villages of Hampton, Yorktown and Williamsburg. Forests covered most of the land. None of the big colonial plantations of such early settlers as the Ludwells, Digges, Carys and Nelsons survived into the 19th century.

The most prominent Peninsula landholders were the Lees, who settled in the 17th century in York and then spread into James City, Warwick and Elizabeth City counties. The family's brick house Kiskiack, which dates from the 1600s, stands abandoned within the Naval Weapons Station. The Peninsula Lees were not members of the famous Lee family of Westmoreland County—the, Lees that produced Robert E. Lee. But they were prominent, too.

The Peninsula clan stayed on this Peninsula and intermarried with other local families such as the Iveys. The best-known of the Peninsula Lees was Richard Decatur Lee, who built the handsome brick house called Lee Hall Manor from 1848 to 1859, giving that "Lee Hall" name to the nearby Chesapeake & Ohio Railway stop. You can see the Lee Hall house close to Route 60.

Richard Decatur Lee was a rich man by 19th-century standards. He built Lee Hall Manor for $10,000 he made from one season's tobacco crop. He placed his home on a knoll in the middle of a grove of oak trees, which still stand. The trees survived from the burning of an earlier house.

Unfortunately, the C&O chose as its 1881 right-of-way the side yard of Lee Hall Manor, cutting in two a tract that once numbered 3,000 acres.

Two other onetime Lee houses survive within Fort Eustis, largely unknown by historians. One is Magnolia House, quarters of the commanding officer of the Army Transportation Command, which was built in 1866 by William Lee, a kinsman of Richard, on the James River near Mulberry Island. (An earlier house on the site had been destroyed in the Civil War.)

In 1871 William Lee sold his farm to agents of Collis Huntington's Old Dominion Land Company which, in 1908, sold off 592 waterfront acres and the house to Charles W. Bailey, a Philadelphia jeweler who had moved to Newport News.

Bailey added to the Lee house and used it as a summer home and hunting lodge. After holding it 10 years, he sold the house and 592 acres for

Glimpses of Tidewater Life   69

Fort Eustis Museum

Peninsulans built Fort Crafford at Mulberry Island to repel Union ships on James.

Virginia Gazette

Kiskiack is 17th century Lee house in Navy Weapons Station, abandoned but still erect.

$90,000 to the Army as part of Fort Eustis in 1918. The house was once called Bailey's Bungalow but is now known as Magnolia House.

Another Peninsula Lee estate in Civil War times was Big Oaks Farm, also within Fort Eustis and now the residence of the Transportation Corps' second-in-command. It is believed to have been owned by Richard Decatur Lee (old Warwick County records were burned in the Civil War and thus information is limited).

The same wealthy Richard Lee also owned Lee's Mill, once a corn-grinding mill next to Lee Hall.

After Appomattox, Richard Decatur Lee was forced to sell his Lee Hall Manor and most other holdings and to move with his wife, Martha, into Big Oaks.

From the Lee heirs, the late J.M. Dozier, onetime secretary of the Old Dominion Land Com-

70 *Along Virginia's Golden Shores*

pany, bought Big Oaks in 1915 and added to it. Like his neighbor Charles Bailey, Dozier sold out to the Army in 1918 to create Fort Eustis, receiving $43,000 for his 481 acres that ran from the Warwick River in Newport News almost to Fort Eustis' present Washington Boulevard, its main street.

Because it was cleared land, the Dozier farm was chosen by the Amy to be the center of Fort Eustis. The farmhouse became the quarters in 1918 of Eustis' commanding officer, Maj. Gen. Archibald Sunderland. Over the years it has been expanded and modernized several times.

Several other Lee family farms were bought by C&O agents in the 1860s and 1870s in preparation for the extension of the railroad down the Peninsula. They were owned by William Lee, Robert E. Lee and Thomas W. Lee, and all were located below what is now 50th Street in present Newport News. But of all their lands, the Lees' most historic was Big Oaks Farm. It was part of a 1,000-acre tract given by the British crown in 1618 to Gov. Sir George Yeardley of Jamestown.

Named Stanley Hundred, it became a 17th-century plantation. The onetime Lees Landing on the Warwick River (close to the present Fort Eustis Officers' Club) appears on early Virginia maps and was used by ships carrying tobacco to European ports. It was later a dock for river boats plying the James.

When Fort Crafford was built by Confederates on Mulberry Island to prevent Federal ships from ascending the James to Richmond (it proved ineffective), nearby farms of the Lees were fortified. Their earthworks, largely built by slave labor in 1861–62, are still identifiable along the James.

Fort Eustis Museum

William Lee built in 1866 on James near Mulberry Island, now residence of Fort Eustis commander.

York Confederate Thomas Phillips defied Yankee blockade in Civil War.

Owen Phillips

22. *A Lone Confederate Hero*

SOUTHERNERS grow up amid glorious legends of the heroic Confederate army, but little is said about the Confederate navy. The fact is that after a few early successes attacking the Northern commerce in 1862 and 1863, the few Confederate warships were driven from the seas by Yankee frigates and gunboats.

Federal control of Peninsula waters in the Civil War was seriously challenged only once, in March 1862, when the Confederate ship *Virginia*, formerly the *Merrimack*, battled the USS *Monitor* in Hampton Roads.

Throughout the Civil War, Federal blockade ships patrolled the James and the York rivers. In the summer of 1862, Harrison's Landing, now called Berkeley plantation, was a major Federal port because the Army of the Potomac was encamped there.

Federal control of shipping on the James River extended as far upstream as Drewry's Bluff in Henrico County. There a Confederate fort dominated a narrow span of the river and prevented Yankee gunboats from getting through and reaching Richmond.

Federal ships on the James River neutralized the effects of the Confederate Navy Yard on the James River at Richmond. There the Confederacy built several ships but was unable to send them into action because of the concentration of waiting Federal warships below Drewry's Bluff.

Among the Confederate sailors from the Peninsula was Thomas Phillips, a York County skipper. He was captured by a Federal warship in the Atlantic Ocean off the Carolina coast in January 1863, while he was trying to run the Yankee blockade with a cargo of provisions sent from Nassau in the Caribbean.

The incident was reported in an official dispatch by Lieutenant Commander William T. Truxtun, who commanded the USS gunboat *Chocura* to enforce the Federal blockade of the Chesapeake. Unfortunately, many Confederate blockade runners were similarly caught by Yankees as they attempted to reach Southern ports, usually on moonless nights, when blockade-running was easiest.

Truxtun reported capturing the York County seaman in a dispatch to his superior, Acting Rear Admiral S.P. Lee, on January 21, 1863. Phillips was captured while commanding the schooner *Pride* with a cargo of 175 sacks of salt plus medical drugs and shoes, all badly needed in the Confederacy.

Peninsula descendants of Capt. Phillips own a copy of Truxtun's dispatch describing their ancestor's capture. It occurred about 15 miles southeast of Frying Pan Shoals, off Cape Hatteras, North Carolina.

Reported Truxtun: "As soon as she [Phillips' schooner *Pride*] discovered this vessel [USS *Chocura*] to be in chase of her, she made sail. The master, Thomas Phillips, on being asked why he was laying off the point of the shoals under easy sail with a fair wind blowing for his assumed port of destination [Baltimore], replied he wished to keep to windward."

Phillips, then only 25, was placed by the Navy in confinement aboard one of its ships and sent northward for trial and punishment. The rest of the crew were sent to Washington, D.C., along with the seized ship.

Phillips' story was told by his grandson, Owen Phillips of Newport News.

I learned that Thomas Phillips grew up around Poquoson as a seagoing man serving chiefly aboard schooners and other vessels operating between Yorktown and Baltimore. When Virginia seceded from the Union in 1861, he enlisted with the York Rangers and served until needed by the Confederacy as a blockade runner.

Phillips survived the war to return to Poquoson and spend his life as a York River waterman and as sheriff. For years he commanded a larger schooner sailing the Chesapeake.

In his obituary in the *Daily Press* on October 14, 1915, he was described as "a brave soldier, a fine officer and a man that was liberal with his money to a fault. He had friends by the hundred, as was shown by the fact that for 25 years he had held the position of sheriff and never anyone had a chance to run against him during that time."

The obituary noted that Phillips "was known to everybody in York County as 'Capt. Tom.'"

A Hampton newspaper, the *Monitor*, wrote of him in 1915: "He is readily accounted the most prominent citizen in the historic county of York."

Owen Phillips

Newport News paper carried headline stories of Phillips' illness, death in October 1915.

23. *The Steamboat Age*

THE JAMES RIVER in the steamboat days of the early century was very much like that bigger Western river that Mark Twain made famous in *Life on the Mississippi*. Daily life along each waterway centered on the arrivals of the big, white riverboats that brought passengers and cargo to enliven the backwoods river communities.

I've been reading about James River's boats in *Plantation on the James* by Ransom B. True of Weyanoke, an 18th-century plantation in Charles City County owned by generation of the Lewis, Douthat, and Harwood families. It is currently the property of Lawrence Lewis Jr. of Richmond, who has rebought the family estate.

Like other James River plantations, Weyanoke depended greatly on its wharf on the James. There those Norfolk-to-Richmond boats stopped to bring mail to the Weyanoke post office. It was one of about two dozen stops that riverboats made on their two-day progress up the James. For years there was a "day boat" and a "night boat," lasting to the 1920s, when I remember them.

Mariner's Museum

SS Glen Cove, *speedy James River sidewheeler of the 1850s, was an early Virginia steamer.*

74   *Along Virginia's Golden Shores*

Daily Press

Norfolk aerial view in 1918 shows Old Bay liner at right, loading up for Baltimore trip.

"The steamboats were the main attraction at the Weyanoke wharf," True writes. "During their heyday on the river—the years from 1815 to 1920—perhaps one hundred or more different steamers called at Weyanoke Wharf."

The earliest James River steamboats, based on Robert Fulton's first successful *Clermont* operation in 1807, were side-wheelers. These picturesque ships abound in Civil War photos of Tidewater, but the wooden sidewheels proved two fragile and were eventually replaced by one or more metal underwater propellers.

By the beginning of the 20th century nearly all James River steamboats were propeller-driven. I remember the ones that called at Pier A in Newport News when I was a boy, both on their upriver and downriver voyages. In the 1920s, when I roamed the James at North End, the "night boat" to Richmond chugged up the James past our house nightly about 7 o'clock.

Besides stopping at Newport News, the boats visited Mulberry Island (now Fort Eustis), Carter's Grove, Jamestown, Scotland Wharf, CIaremont, Ferguson's Wharf, Brandon, Westover, and Harrison's Landing, or Berkeley. Some stops were signalled from shore by a flag run up on a halyard.

Sometimes to save time, passengers boarded the ship in midstream from a rowboat. An English visitor to Weyanoke once wrote, "I then crossed to the north side of the James River, being rowed out at sunrise far from shore to wait for a steamer. The hour of her arrival being somewhat uncertain, we remained for some time in the cold. . . . At length we gladly hailed a large steamer as she came down rapidly toward us, and my baggage was immediately taken care of by two of the crew."

A famous James steamer was the *Ariel*, owned by the Virginia Steamboat Company, which served off and on from 1878 to 1904. Built in Wilmington, Delaware, in 1858, she was one of the first iron-hulled passenger ships of her time.

The best-remembered James River tripper was the *Pocahontas,* known as "Poky," which operated from Richmond to Norfolk from 1893 till 1919. Once she partly burned at Richmond but was rebuilt. Then an engineers' strike ended her river run. She was sold to a New Jersey firm and served in the New York area until scrapped about 1935.

A *Pocahontas* passenger paid only $1.50 to travel the river, with meals costing 60 cents more. She sailed from Richmond on Monday, Wednesday and Friday at 6 A.M. and arrived at Norfolk at 7:30 P.M. She left Norfolk at 6 A.M. on Tuesday, Thursday and Saturday to go back to Richmond.

The *Pocahontas* boasted an electric organ plus bridal chambers, card parlors and many staterooms. When the Old Dominion Line sold her in 1919, several successors tried to use steamboats, but the advent of autos doomed them all by 1924.

Describing "Poky's" arrival at Weyanoke plantation, Ransom True writes, "When she approached Weyanoke, Captain Graves or any of the innumerable small boys to whom he gave permission would pull the *Pochontas's* unique three-note whistle. Sounding across the river, the notes formed a chord long remembered by river dwellers. She would pull up to the wharf. Then she would embark or debark passengers and all types of freight."

The decline of river life came swiftly after Henry Ford put America on wheels in the 1920s. Today the James sees little shipping except for oilers, timber and gravel barges, duck-hunters' bateaux, and summer pleasure craft. The dock at Weyanoke today is dismantled, like those of all other one-time stops of the *Ariel* and the *Pocahontas.* We can only imagine what it once was like.

Daily Press

Pocahontas *and* Jamestown *provided Norfolk-to-Richmond service until 1930s, stopping at plantations.*

24. *Ships to Subdue Spain*

NEWPORT NEWS is a city built by wars. It got its first boost with the Spanish-American War, doubled in size during World War I and grew to be Virginia's fourth largest "wonder city" during World War II.

Americans know little about the Spanish-American War, but it marked the start of the United States' century-long buildup to be the world's military power. Teddy Roosevelt's "bully little war" against Spanish imperialism in Cuba had a big impact on the nation and especially on the infant shipyard in Newport News and the coastal defense base at Fort Monroe.

The conflict started in 1898 after Spain's Cuban colony revolted and Spain sent an army and a fleet to quell the insurrection. The United States, upholding the Monroe Doctrine, came to the aid of the Cubans. After the American battleship *Maine* was sunk in Havana harbor on February 14, 1898, the United States prepared for war with Spain, yet war wasn't formally declared until April.

Many men from Hampton, Newport News and Williamsburg were mustered into service to fight in Cuba. Most Hamptonians fought with Company D, 4th Virginia Infantry, while Newport News volunteers became the Huntington Rifles. The Rifles encamped for months along the James River to protect Newport News against invasion.

The shipyard rushed to completion its first battleships, the USS *Kearsarge* and the USS *Kentucky*. They were launched March 24, 1898, as 18,000 people watched. At the same time the Army took over the Chesapeake & Ohio Railway's piers at Newport News to serve as a port of embarkation for troops. The same thing happened during two World Wars.

Fearing a possible attack by Spanish ships, military officials laid an underwater, electrically controlled mine field across the entrance to Hampton Roads between Old Point and Willoughby Spit. And powerful new coast artillery guns were installed at Fort Monroe, called "the Gibraltar of the Chesapeake." Many Peninsula inductees thought the war sounded exciting, but they were soon bored by delays in moving south to Cuba. Members of the Peninsula Guards were sent to Jacksonville for training, where they were when hostilities ended in July.

Six months later—in December 1898—the members of Company D, 4th Virginia Infantry, reached Cuba to serve as part of the American

Glimpses of Tidewater Life 77

occupation force. They stayed only until February 1899 and came home to a heroes' welcome and were mustered out. They suffered only one fatality, caused by sickness. Newport News ships played a big part in the naval war. The U.S. Navy gunboat *Nashville,* which fired the war's first shot on April 22, 1898, was built at the shipyard. Other locally built warships were part of Admiral William T. Sampson's fleet that defeated the Spanish fleet off Cuba on July 3, 1898.

Then American troops invaded Puerto Rico and met little opposition. They were commanded by Major General Nelson A. Miles who, after the Civil War, served as the commander of Fort Monroe. As such, he was responsible for the security of Jefferson Davis, president of the Confederacy, imprisoned there.

During the summer of 1899, a yellow fever epidemic broke out at the Old Soldiers' Home at Phoebus—presumably started among soldiers who had returned from Cuba. The *Daily Press* of August 1 bore this headline: "A Dreaded Visitor—Yellow Fever Makes Its Appearance at the Old Soldiers' Home—40 Veterans Stricken. Families fled Hampton and Newport News." A C&O train departed Old Point at 3 A.M. bearing

Painting by L. Shafter from *Daily Press*

Battleship Maine exploded in Havana harbor in 1898 to set off United States war with Spain.

300 hysterical passengers, followed by another from Phoebus. *Harper's Weekly* for August 12, 1899, carried a picture labeled "The Exodus from Newport News Caused by the Yellow Fever Outbreak."

Old Point was quarantined, and no one from Phoebus and Hampton could enter. Newport News closed its doors, barricading roads and trolley lines.

Twenty-two people died at the Soldiers' Home before the epidemic subsided and the quarantine was lifted. The Chamberlin Hotel reopened its doors, and refugees came back to the Peninsula from Richmond. Although the Spanish-American War was brief, it marked the beginning of an American arms buildup which reached its height in the Cold War.

Yes, the Peninsula began an arms buildup in the Spanish-American War. Now, with the relaxation of the Cold War, the build-down has begun. It will change Tidewater life.

Painting by F. Cresson Shell from *Daily Press*

Battleships Kentucky *and* Kearsarge *were launched at Newport News in 1898 to fight Spain.*

25. *Oysters and Violence*

MY FIRST BEAT as a reporter for the Newport News papers after I graduated from college in 1937 was the Hampton Roads waterfront. Those were the years of the romantic ballad, "I Cover the Waterfront," and I thought of it as I hustled with my notepad from the newspaper office on Twenty-fifth Street down to the C&O piers on the James River, then bustling with ships discharging bauxite, rubber, coffee, and bananas and loading tobacco, cattle and lots of coal.

I miss that earthy bustle when I visit lower Newport News now.

Ships of every nation called there then, and seamen lit up the dock area with nightly revels that sometimes landed them in jail. Prohibition quieted things eventually.

Part of my beat was the Virginia Commission of Fisheries office at Twenty-fourth Street and West Avenue where a pious Eastern Shoreman named G. Walter Mapp tried to save Virginia's fisheries with a small fleet of police boats. Oysters were still numerous and profitable, and G. Walter had his hands full to avert hostilities between rival Virginia and Maryland "arstermen" or "sea Ayrabs," as the papers called them.

Those were the days of gun-slinging Chesapeake oyster wars, and the frequent violence and death were front-page news. Alas, today the decline of the oyster industry has nearly ended oystering and its wars. As biologists had predicted, years of over-dredging have reduced supplies of the "luscious bivalve." In the past five years

Virginia Division of Tourism

A Tangier oysterman heads out for a day's tonging despite steady decline in catch.

the spread of oyster diseases has nearly finished them.

Mapp's fisheries commission strove hard to bring peace; he was an earnest and peaceful man. He was abetted by the commission's able lawyer, B. Drummond Ayres, who also came from the Eastern Shore. Ayres' son, B.D. Junior, is a top correspondent of *The New York Times.*

The oyster wars tumbled on for 50 years, a tragic era. Watermen are a tough, resentful lot, and they don't like government "meddling." For years after the Civil War they plied their trade with few controls by Virginia and Maryland, who share the bay's fisheries under an agreement signed in 1785. But when over-aggressive oystering in the 1870s threatened the oyster supply, both states began imposing laws to reduce the oyster season, to forbid the taking of small oysters and to control oyster "drudging," as the watermen called it.

Despite the so-called Potomac Compact of 1785, bad blood was inevitable between watermen of the two states. For one thing, Maryland had earlier and harsher controls, which upset Maryland watermen. Virginia followed a more laissez-faire policy for awhile and then in 1875 created a Commission of Fisheries, to be later headquartered in Newport News.

In 1968 the commission was succeeded by the Marine Resources Commission, still located in downtown Newport News. Today its 160 employees are scattered over Tidewater, roughly half in Newport News and others as sea-going fisheries patrolmen. By the time I encountered the oyster wars in 1937, the worst were over. By that time the two states had stronger laws and more patrolmen to enforce them. Soon to back up conservation efforts would come the Virginia Institute of Marine Science at Gloucester Point, a research arm of The College of William and Mary.

Many gripes have fed the anger of Chesapeake watermen over the years. It's hard for fishermen to know which underwater area belongs to Virginia and which to Maryland. Or which oyster grounds are public, to be used by all licensed watermen, or private, to be dredged only by the dredger who paid rent for it.

To make matters worse, equipment that oystermen were permitted by the two states to use has sometimes differed, adding to the difficulties of enforcement. "Arstering is the only trade in the world that forbids the use of modern equipment," complained a grizzled waterman at one hearing.

In George Walter Mapp's day, fisheries laws were enforced by a small fleet of motorboats. Seaplanes were introduced later.

A tragedy in 1949 that worsened relations between the two states was the shooting of Earl Nelson, a 60-year-old Crisfield waterman, by Virginia fisheries deputy David Acree. Acree had spotted Nelson's Maryland boat crabbing two miles inside the Virginia boundary, landed his seaplane beside Nelson, and ordered him to steer his craft to a Virginia patrol boat. Acree's rifle accidentally went off as the two scuffled, and Nelson was fatally injured.

At last in the 1980s the collapse of Chesapeake oystering finally occurred. Parasitical diseases spread over the oyster bottoms of the Chesapeake, brought on by years of light spring

Author's collection

Sturdy oyster "buy boats" line up in Hampton River, hoping for better oyster catches.

rains, which increased the salinity of bay waters at a crucial time in the oyster's lifespan. Fortunately, the Chesapeake's supplies of crabs and of some fish seem to be holding up better despite man's greed.

When I go back to the waterfront today, everything is changed. I hope the Marine Resources Commission can preserve and increase what's left of our once-abundant bay fisheries.

Daily Press

Chesapeake sailing skipjack was familiar all-purpose workboat until power boats took over.

26. *When Pier A Flourished*

ONE OF THE BUSIEST spots in early Newport News of the 1920s and '30s was the long wooden dock at 25th Street and the James River, called Pier A. That's where water taxis operated to carry crewmen and pilots back from their James River anchorage to shore. And that's where the produce of James River farmers and fishermen was sold, wholesale and retail, from the decks of river boats to customers on the dock.

What wonderful things Pier A's boatmen sold. There were cured hams, shoulders, and side meat from across the river, in Nansemond and Isle of Wight counties. There were dandoodles—long strings of black-smoked sausage you split and fried for breakfast (we didn't know cholesterol then) or split and cooked with turnip greens to give it flavor. There were chickens, ducks, geese, turkeys, and cleaned muskrats and possums. And there were all kinds of fruits and vegetables, depending on the season. It was a gourmand's heaven.

Even more important, Pier A was the terminus for the Old Dominion Steamship Company's big passenger steamer *Hampton Roads,* plying between Smithfield, Newport News and Norfolk. It also berthed Captain A.F. Jester's small but feisty mail-boat, *Oneita,* which competed with the *Hampton Roads*.

A 1920s photo shows mounds of watermelons on the dock and a string of produce boats alongside. In the background are the Casino and a part of the Post Office nearby at 25th Street and West Avenue.

Until the James River Bridge opened in 1928,

Daily Press

Produce boats await Pier A customers, with a steam yacht and schooner offshore in James River.

Glimpses of Tidewater Life 83

Daily Press

Produce boats lie along Pier A in 1910 photo by George Barclay. Postoffice is in background.

my family and other residents of southern Virginia crossed by boat from Newport News to Battery Park and Smithfield. The rise of autos and bridges in the 1930s bankrupted ship companies operating on the Chesapeake's rivers and creeks. Today only a handful of gravel and oil firms operate tugs and barges on the James.

I well remember boarding the Smithfield boat in the 1920s. It arrived at Pier A from Norfolk about 4 P.M. and took cargo and passengers. Stevedores hurriedly pushed or carried cargo aboard—autos, farm equipment, hardware and groceries. My parents held us children tightly till we were safely on the passenger deck, looking down.

My parents knew the captain and the purser, who punched our tickets. In fact, they seemed to know nearly everybody, for the boat *Hampton Roads* operated from Smithfield, and its officers were important men in the tiny 1920s town. My family had moved to Newport News in 1918, but they returned with their children to their birthplace for weekends, holidays and vacations. A lot of other Southsiders who'd moved to Newport News during World War I also traveled the boat.

The trip up the James and into Pagan River to Smithfield took a little more than an hour and got you there by supper time. My brothers and I happily ran around the decks with our dog while we waited for the loud ship's whistle and the captain's loud "All a-a- a-a-b-b-o-o-o-a-r-r-r-d."

Once she set sail, she passed close to the Warwick Machine Shop pier, now torn down, and skirted the shipyard before moving up the river off our familiar North End shoreline. Several miles further along, she made the port turn past

Eclipse and then up the winding Pagan to the village of Battery Park. When we reached Smithfield's Red Point, the captain blew his "Here-I-Come" whistle to let his wife put supper on the table.

The *Hampton Roads* and her competitor, the *Oneita,* were Smithfield's only commercial ties with the world before autos, for the town had no railroad. In the old days, before 1875, a sailing schooner had moved the town's peanuts, cured meat, corn and truck crops. It was the three-masted *Three Sisters,* owned by Captain O.G. Delk and by peanut processor P.D. Gwaltney Sr., father of the P.D. who founded the ham-curing firm.

Then, about 1875, Captain Delk joined the Old Dominion and began to sail its steamboats.

A Smithfield woman named Dorothy Robbins wrote her recollections of the steamers in 1947. "Captain Delk loved his boats," she wrote, "and when the *Isle of Wight,* loaded to the water's edge with peanuts, burned at the dock on a morning in the '90s, he wept like a child."

Dorothy Robbins wrote also of the Sunday school picnics and moonlight excursions the Smithfield boat also made. Its dining room served breakfast en route to Newport News in the morning, "crisply fried oysters or Ocean View spots, Smithfield ham, and scrambled eggs, accompanied by hot biscuits and strong coffee."

My parents recalled Smithfield's Sunday school picnics and moonlight cruises by steamboat back in the horse-and-buggy days. Dorothy Robbins wrote that "The moonlight trips were highly popular with the younger set, and some would bring along guitars to strum while the others sang, but many were content merely to hold hands and listen to the water swish."

Captain Delk was a celebrated figure in Smithfield, for he'd been born there and was kin to the Gwaltneys and other families. While he sailed the *Accomac,* she collided in Hampton Roads with the *Luray,* another James River ship, and sank. However, Captain Delk was exonerated and served the Old Dominion line 26 years, retiring at 62.

When the state of Virginia began to build hard-surfaced highways in the 1920s, trucks took over the water-borne commerce of the James and other rivers. Pier A declined as a passenger and produce center. Finally, the Old Dominion line began to lose money and decided to end its Smithfield service. But the little farm town didn't give up its ship easily. A Smithfield Boat Line was formed under the leadership of John I. Cofer Jr., and Captain Levin Winder was hired as skipper of its last ship, the *Hampton Roads.*

In a few years even the local company had to give up. Smithfield's peanut factories had never recovered from a disastrous 1921 fire, and much of their business moved to Suffolk. The opening of the James River Bridge in 1928 drained further business. My family never sailed on the *Hampton Roads* after 1928 but drove to Smithfield via the bridge.

Pier A lingered on awhile, but today it's gone. The 1920s photograph recalls a colorful landmark of the vanished steamboat era.

Buckroe's onetime merry-go-round now entrances youngsters in renovated downtown Hampton.

Author's collection

27. *Beaches and Bathing Beauties*

THE FAVORITE SITE for Sunday school picnics in eastern Virginia in the early 1900s was Buckroe Beach on the southern shore of the Chesapeake. Today, Buckroe is a residential suburb of Hampton still boasting a swimming beach but sadly shorn of its roller-coaster ride, merry-go-round and "Old Mill Stream" of romantic gondolas pulled by underwater chain.

Buckroe was developed as a public beach and amusement park by James S. Darling of Hampton in 1897, at a time when surf bathing became popular. Buckroe's success led black businessmen to develop the Bay Shore Hotel Company on water frontage near Buckroe. Robert R. Moton of Hampton University was a leader in this, which was said to be the only resort in the South for black people. In that era, Victorian modesty dictated baggy bathing suits, which made swimming difficult. Bathers dressed in waterfront locker rooms.

"There was no mixed bathing in 1900," one Hampton lady recalls. "Males and females were required to bathe separately in roped-off areas. All ladies were required to wear black stockings."

The early beach at Buckroe plantation was chiefly used by fishermen until after the Civil War, when Mrs. Mary Ann Dobbins Herbert opened a boarding house for summer guests. Soon businessman Edward Chiles opened a public bathhouse, and then someone built a pavilion for ballroom dancing. Those were the days of the turkey trot, the Viennese waltz and the fox trot.

When Darling extended his street-car line to Buckroe, he built a big frame Buckroe Beach Hotel facing the shore and added a picnic and dance pavilion and, later, an amusement park. The hotel was managed by Charles Hewins and was famous for fried spot and seafood dinners.

Buckroe's merry-go-round carried millions of happy riders in the 1900s. It has been preserved by the city of Hampton and reinstalled downtown near the air and space museum.

Other small hotels and rooming houses were opened. So were souvenir shops. At the amusement park, concessionaires operated orange juice stands, cotton candy dispensers, saltwater taffy shops and "games of chance and skill." Especially popular were 10-cent games to test one's marksmanship or strength. Prizes were kewpie dolls with brightly colored feather clothing.

Fireworks enlivened the Fourth of July and Labor Day at Buckroe. Peninsula residents came in Model T Fords to picnic with fried chicken and deviled eggs and watch the fireworks.

For the college-age crowd, Buckroe offered dancing on the pavilion, with the Jolly Jazz Orchestra of Newport News playing such hits as "Moonlight Serenade," "Moonglow" and "Three Little Fishes." Tickets were 10 cents a dance or three for a quarter. Girls sometimes danced with each other if boys were shy. Vari-colored lights played on a rotating crystal ball to create moonbeams over the scene.

Who can forget Eddie Travis singing "Button Up Your Overcoat" while donning a huge raccoon coat? The orchestra in those years included musicians like Dick Viancour, Karl Lanier, Charlie Epes, Rouzee Goodman, Gordon Weyburn, Sammy Cohen, Dudie Bowers, Randy Rouse and others. They were in great demand.

Sunday schools were well-attended in those days, partly because they dangled hope of picnic outings to Buckroe for their students. C&O excursion trains rolled into Buckroe all summer, conveying noisy young picnickers to the pavilion and a day full of frenzied sensation before nightfall.

Buckroe's success attracted families to buy land at the beach and build cottages. Further along the bay, a family style beach called Grandview developed after 1890, when the tiny Grandview Hotel was built there. A dance pavilion came later, where young Ella Fitzgerald of Newport News sang with a band before she hit the big time. Like Buckroe, Grandview has developed into year-round suburbia today.

Buckroe then offered some of the fun of

Daily Press

After Buckroe was built by trolley interests in 1897, beach bathing flowered.

today's theme parks, like Busch Gardens, although it was a lot cheaper. Kids were crazy about it.

But styles change, and surfbathing declined after swimming pools grew common. Then, too, more stinging nettles invaded Chesapeake Bay, making Buckroe waters less pleasant. Buckroe was heavily damaged in the 1933 hurricane and never recovered.

But chiefly, Buckroe folded because Peninsula vacationers sought newer attractions. The dance hall, the 10-cent rides, and kewpie doll games seemed tame to guys who'd invaded Sicily, Saipan and Iwo Jima.

Buckroe had passed its heyday by the 1950s, when crowds swarmed there on summer weekends.

Daily Press

28. *Storms, Hurricanes and Earthquakes*

WHEN THE ENGLISH settled Virginia, they were shocked to learn how hot the summer got and how violent were the thunderstorms. And, during the 18th century, they also learned about three other threats: autumnal hurricanes, spring floods of upland rivers (particularly the James and the Potomac) and earthquakes.

Earthquakes?

Yes, earthquakes. The Seismological Observatory for Virginia, which is part of Virginia Tech at Blacksburg, compiles records of earthquake tremors reported in Virginia as far back as 1774. There have been at least 131 earthquakes, most of them in the Piedmont section of the state around Charlottesville.

Hurricanes and floods have been Tidewater's chief natural calamities over the years. The hurricanes have been felt especially along the coast, after high winds have raised water levels and bombarded the Chesapeake with mountainous waves. They were numerous in Hampton Roads early this century, reaching their peak in Hurricane Agnes in August 1933. Flooding of the James at Richmond has also been frequent, usually in spring after upland rains. A floodwall is now expected to limit flood damage.

Daily Press

Richmond's 14th Street Bridge, foreground, is inundated in 1985 James River flood.

Frank Leslie's Illustrated Newspaper

In 1877, James River flood inundated Richmond's lower Main Street at great loss to stores and homes.

Apparently no really destructive earthquake has ever shaken Virginia. However, equipment for precisely measuring quake intensity, like the Richter Scale, has not been available until recent years.

VPI's Seismological Observatory is part of a chain of earthquake reporting centers around the nation. Two of its scientists have compiled two listings of recorded Virginia quakes, one covering the years 1774 to 1900 and the other from 1900 to 1974.

The first recorded earthquake in Virginia occurred at 2 in the afternoon of February 21, 1774. It was a relatively big one, drawing reports from six localities in Virginia and one from North Carolina, embracing 58,000 square miles. At Westover plantation on the James River in Charles City County, someone in the household of William Byrd III reported: "Last Monday, about two o'clock, a smart shock of an earthquake was felt . . . which shook the dwelling house very much."

It was felt also in Williamsburg, Richmond, Petersburg, Fredericksburg and Charlottesville. At Monticello, an unidentified correspondent—Thomas Jefferson, perhaps?—wrote "two violent earthquake shocks" were felt on February 21, 1774, and another the next day.

Someone in Petersburg, commenting on an earlier report from Richmond, added: "The motion of the earth [in the February 21 earthquake] was still greater [than in Richmond], many houses having been moved considerably off their foundations, and the inhabitants so much alarmed as to run out of doors." In Fredericksburg, the quake "shook the glasses on the table, etc. and terrified the inhabitants greatly, but no bad consequences attended it."

The shock was felt 300 miles from Tidewater in Salem, North Carolina, where it caused "all the bells hanging in the store to ring, but was not noticed by all the people."

Two days after the February 21 earthquake, a strong aftershock was felt in Williamsburg. One resident reported, "On Wednesday night there was a violent tremor of the earth."

The VPI earthquake data lists no other Tidewater quake until December 31, 1816. A report from Norfolk on that date says, "Several of our citizens . . . felt a shock here." On the same day a ship on the Atlantic near Norfolk "experienced a very severe shock of an earthquake, which was accompanied by a noise so much resembling that of a vessel when striking on a rock or wreck—that they for some time believed it actually to be the case."

The most extensive earthquake in Virginia's history occurred March 9, 1828, felt and reported from Philadelphia southward to Raleigh, including Smithfield, Norfolk, Petersburg and Richmond.

In the White House, President John Quincy Adams recorded in his diary:

> There was this evening the shock of an earthquake, the first which I ever distinctly noticed at the moment when it happened. I was writing in this book, when the table began to shake under my hand and the floor under my feet.... It continued about two minutes, then ceased. It was about 11 at night. I immediately left writing, and went to my bed-chamber, where my wife was in bed, much alarmed.

Five years later, in 1833, another strong quake shook Piedmont. At Dover, in Goochland, 42 miners were killed when a coal pit buried them. In Charlottesville, Jeffersons' granddaughter wrote:

> We had the most severe shock from an earthquake yesterday morning that had ever been experienced before.... The windows rattled violently, and I began to fear the chimney might be shaken off. When it had reached its height it gradually diminished.

In 1897, Newport News was rocked by a quake on May 31, at 1:38 in the afternoon, that "frightened a great many people," according to VPI records. It was worst "near the edge of the water, where it caused the piers and buildings to rock," though without damage. In Norfolk and Portsmouth, householders, feeling the shock "rushed into the streets panic stricken."

The shock's center was in Giles County, but it was felt also in West Virginia, Kentucky, North and South Carolina, Tennessee and Ohio.

The last significant Virginia earthquake of record was on December 11, 1969, centering around Richmond but felt as far away as Roanoke and upper North Carolina.

Seismologists believe earthquake fault lines are created by subterranean pressures caused by the shift of huge "plates" beneath the earth. Fortunately for Virginians, no active fault lines seem apt to disturb Virginia's tranquility in the foreseeable future. It's those August and autumnal hurricanes that we coastal Virginians have to worry about.

Daily Press

Richmond has often been flooded by the James, as it was in this 1870 photograph.

29. *Land of "The Life Worth Living"*

GLOUCESTER COUNTY never had a better press agent than Thomas Dixon Jr., a novelist and later a Hollywood producer who lived and wrote at Elmington plantation from 1899 to 1905. Dixon's effusive description of Tidewater, published in 1905 as *The Life Worth Living,* attracted many others to live along the shore of the Chesapeake Bay and its tributaries in those leisurely steamboat days.

Tom Dixon also wrote the powerful novel, *The Clansman,* while he lived in Gloucester. In 1915, David Wark Griffith made it into the movie, "The Birth of a Nation."

During his lifetime, Dixon was a Baptist preacher, attorney, actor, theater critic and Democratic officeholder. Although he made over $1.2 million, he died nearly penniless in Raleigh, North Carolina, in 1946 at the age of 82.

In Gloucester, tales survive of Dixon's six years as owner of Elmington on the North River, now the stately vacation home of German industrialist Peter Glasel. Dixon bought it on an impulse to get his wife and three children out of New York City, where they had moved 12 times in 11 years.

To buy Elmington and its 500 lordly acres,

Library of Congress

Thomas Dixon Jr. wrote "The Life Worth Living" when he lived in Gloucester.

91

Gloucester Courthouse, shown about 1920, was beginning to be mechanized in Thomas Dixon's day.

Dixon had to sell his brownstone row house on New York's West 94th Street, near Central Park. Property in Gloucester was dirt cheap in those days. Dixon was amazed at all the cleared fields and woodland—and the steamboat dock—he got in exchange for his ugly New York house. With another $1,000 or so, he added two-story columns to the brick Elmington mansion, built years earlier by the Tabb family and considered one of the finest in Gloucester. The house had 32 rooms. Nearby lived many old landed families, all impoverished by the Civil War: the Seldens, Taliaferros, Pages, Dimmocks, Catletts, Perrins and others.

Reading *The Life Worth Living* today, I get the impression that Dixon had a noveaux-riche desire to immerse his young wife and three children in the innocent rural life he'd known as a Baptist preacher's son in Shelby, North Carolina.

"We moved to Tidewater, Virginia, the home of John Smith, the oldest settlement in America and yet the most primitive, the most beautiful, and least known spot in our continent," he wrote at the beginning of *The Life Worth Living*. He was attracted by the 200-year-old site, the huge elms and the plantings of fruits, berries and other garden and greenhouse edibles.

In those days the Chesapeake area was knit by steamboats and produce schooners, and Elmington had "an artistic little pier which gives us daily mail and traffic with Old Point and Norfolk and the outside world," Dixon wrote. "Around us on the beautiful . . . North River we see from our porch 14 waterfront homes." He and his sons loved sailing, duck-hunting, fishing and crabbing.

Dixon wrote of collecting diamond-back terrapin, then a Virginia delicacy; of crabs and clams "so plentiful they are considered a very plebeian diet," and of towering Elmington itself "built by Dr. John Prosser Tabb, at that time the richest and most influential man in the county."

Dixon enjoyed spending money, and he bought horses, cows and boats, meanwhile improving Elmington. "It only required the addition on both sides of the Greek facades with the pillars," he writes. "I put in a system of sewerage into Tidewater [the North River]. An acetylene gas plant gives us finer lights than electricity. . . . We rummaged through the junk shops of New York and dragged out a complete set of massive brass chandeliers."

The Dixons enjoyed neighbors, but Dixon himself spent most of his time in his log cabin office near the shore, writing novels. In 1902 he published *The Leopard's Spots,* in 1905 *The Clansman,* and in 1907 *The Traitor.* They made a hit with Southern readers, for they played on fears that interracial marriage threatened the integrity of the races.

As a deterrent, Dixon in his books favored the Ku Klux Klan and its segregationism. Alas, the pull of fame in 1905 drew Tom Dixon away from "The Life Worth Living" and back to New York City.

Ever the zealot, Dixon in 1915 organized his own Hollywood studio and produced five films, including "The Fall of a Nation." However, Dixon's career declined during World War I. By 1919 he was penniless.

Looking back on his turbulent life, gadfly Tom Dixon must have wished he had heeded the desires of his wife and children in 1905 and stayed in Gloucester, True, he gained celebrity, but he died a poor and disillusioned man.

How much better might he and his family fared had he resisted the lure of riches and stuck to "The Life Worth Living."

Thomas Dixon Jr. lived at Elmington from 1899 to 1905 and added columns to the North River mansion.

Daily Press

30. *Jamestown Celebrates in 1907*

IN 1907, Tidewater played host to an influx of visitors for the Jamestown Exposition celebrating the 300th anniversary of English settlement of North America. Particularly involved were Jamestown and Williamsburg, which received unprecedented numbers of tourists, and Norfolk, which was chosen as the site for a World's Fair extravaganza.

The exposition, sponsored by the federal and state governments, cost a fortune, but it helped put Virginia's historic sites on the map. The Norfolk exposition grounds and its buildings on Hampton Roads were later taken over by the Navy.

Not many folks are alive to recall Jamestown as it was in 1907. One of them is Margaret Leal Work of McLean, whose grandfather was custodian for the Association for the Preservation of Virginia Antiquities at Jamestown. Mrs. Work remembers those years well and writes about them in a sturdy script.

Her grandfather, William Leal, was a Richmond stone mason who came to Jamestown in 1907 to help erect the commemorative monument on the island. For a while, he and daughter "roughed it" in a temporary cabin. Later, when he was custodian for the APVA, he lived in the Yeardley House, which was built on the island at the time of the exposition.

"My father brought me there in 1907 for the Tricentennial," Mrs. Work reports, and "my parents and I lived in a tent for the two weeks we were there. After that the Yeardley House was built, and we had family reunions there every summer until Grandpa's death in 1915. Sometimes I stayed there all summer."

Jamestown then had a public dock for passenger and excursion boats. There President Teddy Roosevelt's yacht, the *Mayflower*, tied up in 1907, and there Lord Bryce, British ambassador to the United States, came ashore to make a speech at the dedication of the granite obelisk.

"Grandpa Leal was the postmaster, sheriff and tour guide," Mrs. Work recalls. "He sold postcards and a few souvenirs to tourists. People came by riverboat—the paddlewheeler *Pocahontas*—or by buggy or carriage from Williamsburg. Occasionally a motor car came—not more than six to 10 visitors a week. There were no accommodations for visitors on the island, or even for the work crew who built the monument and the sea wall."

While working near the church, Mrs. Work reports, "Grandpa unearthed a skeleton of a man.

". . . The graveyard was overgrown. Graves were covered with wood slabs. Names and dates were spelled out by short wood pegs hammered into the slabs."

About the same time Colonel Samuel Yonge and a crew of laborers were building a masonry sea wall to protect Jamestown from further erosion. Yonge discovered several remains of buildings and burials but was prohibited by the APVA from digging within the Confederacy's Civil War fort, laid up on the island in 1862. Not until 1994, was an archaeological study of this area begun.

Young Margaret enjoyed visiting her grandfather at Jamestown. "Often we found Indian beads, arrow heads, pieces of clay pipe, a Confederate or Union bullet, or cut stones that I was told were Indian good luck charms," she recalls. Life on Jamestown was quiet, except during the summer of the Exposition year.

"Light was by kerosene lamps. Windows were covered with cheesecloth, but gnats got through and swarmed around the lamps till they caught fire. Usually the lamps were thrown out the window aflame to prevent damage to the house."

Near the Yeardley House, Mrs. Work recalls,

Margaret Leal, (left) now Mrs. Work, played with friends at Jamestown while visiting her grandpa.

"there was a beautiful garden, originally patterned after the Rolfe garden in England. Chicken wire enclosed it." Later the garden was destroyed by deer which forage over the island. "A family of copperhead snakes lived under the house. I found one in my bed one night," she adds.

Mrs. Work writes: "We lived mostly on the land. Once a week we went to Williamsburg by

James River steamer Pocahontas *lands commemorative excursioners at Jamestown dock in 1907.*

Sightseeing boats gathered at Old Point in February 1909 to watch President Roosevelt review the Great White Fleet.

horse and buggy, over what we called the back road—past the metal gates, over the wooden bridge without guard rails that crossed the back river [the Thoroughfare]. It was a one-lane road. Trees met overhead from each side, so no sun came through. The thick yellow mud was hard to drive through, so the nine-mile trip could take three hours."

Williamsburg then was a muddy village of about 1,500, including about 300 William and Mary students, all male. "While the week's groceries were put in our wagon," Mrs. Work recalls, " we could buy ice cream or visit friends in town. That night and the next day we had fresh meat at Jamestown but could not keep it much longer. The river boat brought a 100 pound block of ice twice a week."

Henry Ford began to make Model Ts in 1908, and the first hard-surfaced road was run from Williamsburg to Jamestown about the same time. "When cars began to come through," Mrs. Work remembers, "the trip to Williamsburg could be hazardous. The horse would panic and rear and gallop. Either the car or horse had to retreat to a side road."

III

The Age of Flight

Weymouth Crumpler

Pilot Hanson Ely flew Curtiss "pusher" from USS Birmingham *at Newport News in 1910.*

31. *The First Carrier Takeoff*

WEYMOUTH CRUMPLER wants the world to know the first airplane takeoff from a ship at sea occurred in Hampton Roads in 1910. "It's a little known fact that the plane took off from the deck of the USS *Birmingham* off Newport News Point and landed safely a few minutes later at Willoughby Spit, on the Norfolk shoreline," says the retired businessman, a member of the Newport News Historical Committee.

Crumpler encouraged the city to place a monument memorializing the event on the Boat Harbor waterfront, reminding the world of the historic flight. It was made by Eugene B. Ely, a civilian stunt pilot who had been born in Davenport, Iowa, and who died a year after his Hampton Roads flight in a crash at Macon, Georgia. Meanwhile, though, he also made the Navy's first successful short-to-ship landing on the West Coast.

Ely's flight was one of many experimental efforts following the Wright brothers' first successful flight at Kitty Hawk, North Carolina, on December 17, 1903. He had learned to fly at Glenn Curtiss's pioneer flying school in New York state in 1909 and had persuaded the Navy to let him fly from a Navy ship the next year.

"This was a world-shaking event," says Crumpler. "It should be of real interest to Newport News and Norfolk and the whole Hampton Roads area."

At Newport News, Ely flew a new experimental Curtiss plane, the Golden Flyer, with double wings and a propeller at its rear, giving it the nickname, "Pusher." The one-man plane was operated from an open cockpit.

Earlier in 1910, inventor Glenn Curtiss had won a *New York World* prize of $10,000 for flying from Albany to New York City. The flight covered 150 miles in two hours and 46 minutes at an average speed of 54.18 miles per hour. Curtiss called his plane the "Albany Flier" for this venture.

Until Ely made his flight, Washington's naval officials had dismissed proposals for flying off Navy ships as "stunts." But Ely won the support of Captain Washington Chambers, the Navy's first director of aviation. Chambers "happened to be bright enough to want to go with it," Crumpler says of Ely's experiment.

For the takeoff from the USS *Birmingham*, the Navy built an 83-foot plywood ramp as a launching platform. The weather was gray that November day, and Ely wanted to fly before it got worse. But the runway was short, and Ely and his plane dipped dangerously as they took off.

"Ely's plane dipped precariously close to the salty, cold Hampton Roads waters," Crumpler says, "but he nudged it aloft and landed at Norfolk's Willoughby Spit area after a five-mile

Weymouth Crumpler

Pioneer "pusher-type" plane was flown in first carrier-type takeoff at Newport News in 1910.

flight." Writing of the incident, ex-curator Louis S. Casey of the National Air and Space Museum in Washington, relates: "Taking off in inclement weather and with the cruiser barely underway, Ely dipped down toward the water, 37 feet below the deck, to gain the necessary flying speed. Recovering barely in time to avoid disaster, Ely did contact the water with his wheels, throwing up a spray that damaged his propeller. With his propeller split, Ely headed for land, Willoughby Spit, and effected a safe landing to complete the first flight from a ship at sea."

Ely and Captain Chambers then persuaded the Navy in 1911 to attempt the first plane landing on a Navy ship. In that case, Ely took off from an Army airfield near San Francisco Bay and landed on the cruiser USS *Pennsylvania,* which had a platform built over her stern. The ship's skipper called it "the most important landing of a bird since the dove flew back to Noah's ark."

When World War I enveloped Europe in 1914 and Canada sought hurry-up flight training for military pilots, Glenn Curtiss remembered Newport News and decided to move his flight school from Buffalo, New York, to this warmer clime. He sent Thomas Scott Baldwin, later an Army Air Corps officer, to the Peninsula early in 1915 to start it.

For the airfield site, Curtiss chose acreage along lower Jefferson Avenue at the Newport News Boat Harbor, later the site of the Army's Camp Stuart after the United States entered the war. In its brief life span Curtiss Field became a pioneer trainer of American and Canadian pilots. One of the first was Buck Gallop, who joined the Army Air Corps, became a war hero in France, and was impersonated by Richard Barthelmess in "The Dawn Patrol," judged the best movie of 1930.

Another Curtiss student was Major William Mitchell, who commuted down the Potomac each weekend from his duty station in Washington to learn to fly. He became General Billy Mitchell, advocate of airpower, who resigned from the Army to protest its reluctance to create a separate air force. Another pioneer was Vernon Castle, famous with his wife Irene for ballroom dancing.

Curtiss Field had well-known flyers as instructors. One was Bert Acosta, who was to serve Richard E. Byrd as pilot on polar expeditions. Another was Victor Carlstrom, who was Curtiss's chief test pilot.

A painting of Ely's 1910 Newport News flight has been created by artist Robert Holland and hangs in the city's municipal building. Weymouth Crumpler has other mementos of the event also in mind. Just you wait.

32. *Boating Along the James*

THE JAMES was far busier in 1911 than it is today. Freight and passenger ships filled Hampton Roads' anchorages, and daily passenger steamers hauled travelers from Tidewater's river towns to such cities as Norfolk, Washington, Baltimore, and New York.

Daily passenger steamers connected Norfolk and Newport News with Richmond, travelling the 60 miles in a little over twelve hours. You could go to sleep in Newport News one night and wake up in Richmond the next morning.

Those river boats—one "day steamer" and one "night steamer"—stopped along the James at any of two dozen docks that happened to have mail, passengers, or freight awaiting movement. Automobiles were few in 1911, but the boats hauled their share of horses and mules.

Among the favorite steamboat stops was Jamestown, whose pier also received excursion steamers loaded with Sunday school trippers from Richmond or from Hampton Roads. Jamestown was a favorite landing, for its 1639 brick church had been rebuilt for the Jamestown Exposition of 1907, and statues of John Smith and Pocahontas had been erected on the waterfront. Lots of people brought George Eastman's new "brownie" cameras, called Kodaks, to take pictures.

To orient 1911 visitors, historian William G. Stanard of Richmond wrote a pamphlet, "Notes for a Journey on the James." It listed the plantations along the river and included a fold-out map of them. It was sold at the Jamestown post office and souvenir stand, operated by the Association for the Preservation of Virginia Antiquities.

Having sailed the lower James many times, I can appreciate Stanard's advice: "As the steamer approaches Jamestown, the tourist's eye is caught by . . . the massive sea-wall erected by the United States Government, which will forever protect the Island. . . ." (Alas, the wall had to be replaced by 1957, but it did save the eroding shoreline.)

Stanard extolled the work of Colonel Samuel Yonge, the U. S. Army engineer who had directed the Army's seawall construction in 1905 and 1906. Yonge also discovered the early statehouse foundations in the course of his digging. Fascinated by Jamestown's archaeology, he stayed on to excavate part of the 22 1/2 acres of the island surrounding the church, which a wealthy Ohioan, Edward E. Barney, had given the APVA in 1893.

Stanard urged readers to buy Yonge's book, *The Site of Old James Towne, 1707–1698,* sold at the APVA shop for $1.25. It was Yonge's story

Daily Press photo by Herb Barnes

At Halfway Creek on the James fishermen empty their trap of catfish, now a prized delicacy.

of his findings, complete with diagrams. It is now long out of print, but to archaeologists it remains a valuable account.

Steaming up the James was a favorite recreation in the days before automobiles seduced America. Boats like the *Ariel* and the *Pocahontas* provided Norfolk-to-Richmond service. I remember seeing them as they docked briefly at Pier A in Newport News in the 1920s, on their way upriver. After awhile, auto transportation would put all these boats out of business.

Stanard described for readers the sights other than Jamestown: Mulberry Island, Burwell's Bay in the Isle of Wight, Carter's Grove, Hog Island, Kingsmill, Archer's Hope, Swan's Point in Surry, Gray's Creek, Four Mile Tree, the Chickahominy, and Sandy Point in Charles City.

Stanard also wrote of the surviving estates between Jamestown and Richmond: Brandon, Weyanoke, Westover, Berkeley, Appomattox Manor, Shirley, Wilton, and Ampthill. The last two were later moved to Richmond and now happily adjoin each other in the Westhampton suburbs, overlooking the James.

The guidebook recites attractions created at Jamestown in 1907 for the Exposition. These include the 1639 church reconstruction, the Smith and Pocahontas statues, and the 1907 Federal monument, dedicated by British Ambassador Lord Bryce. Unfortunately, the latter is a regrettable intrusion amid Jamestown's simple ruins.

The guidebook warns that pilfering of Jamestown brick is forbidden by the APVA. A custodian "will rigidly suppress all disorder and arrest any person guilty of disorderly conduct . . . or injuring buildings, tombs, fences, monuments, ruins, etc.," it warns.

Stanard explains that until Edward E. Barney bought the 1,550-acre island during Reconstruction and began to raise crops, "the tombs and tower had been constantly subject to the vandalism of visitors." He declared that many acres had eroded before the sea wall was built.

Ship transport on the James has declined to almost nothing since those days. Jamestown no longer even has a dock. In fact, most plantation docks have fallen into disuse. River traffic now consists chiefly of oil tankers, newsprint freighters, and barges hauling timber, gravel, and building materials.

But Jamestown remains very much a travel attraction, thanks to fine highways and the attentions of the APVA, state, and federal governments. Extensive exhibits added during the 350th anniversary in 1957 offer much to see. But the old river boats—the *Jamestown, Pocahontas, Brandon,* and other sisters—are long since gone, rotting away in ship graveyards along the Atlantic.

An early photo catches a trotline crabber pulling up his baited line to remove crabs.

Ox-drawn cart unloads bagged grain onto rowboat at Upper Brandon on the James in 1890 photo.

Army's Billy Mitchell was airpower advocate in his lifetime, honored after death.

33. *Billy Mitchell Learns to Fly*

BILLY MITCHELL is a name that looms large in the history of aviation. It was Billy—Army Brigadier General William Mitchell—who tried to convince the Army and Navy in the 1920s that air power was all important militarily. He made such a fuss that he was court-martialed and demoted to colonel. Then he resigned from the Army.

Today many of his ideas are incorporated in the United States Air Force, which became a third arm of American military might after World War II.

Mitchell was a deskbound Army major in Washington before World War I, and he felt the urge to fly. He commuted each weekend by Chesapeake Bay steamer from Washington to Old Point to learn flying at Coast Aeronautical Station at Newport News' Boat Harbor. The field was started to train flyers in 1915 by Glenn Curtiss, a Buffalo, New York, airplane builder.

Much of Mitchell's military experience was at Langley Field, which the Army built in 1917 as a pioneer Air Corps base. He became best known after his 1921 experimental bombing of obsolete ships in the Atlantic Ocean off the Virginia Capes. Most of the hulls were of German warships that had been captured by the U.S. Navy in World War I.

The tests were conducted by Army's First Provisional Air Brigade at Langley Field and Naval Air Service seaplanes from Norfolk. After the German hulls were sunk, planes from Langley Field sank obsolete American battleships.

The bombings proved that aerial bombs could sink even steel war ships. Tough-talking Billy Mitchell felt he had proved the wisdom of creating an aviation arm equal in status to the Army and Navy, and he urged Congress to do so. But his criticism of military leaders for "neglecting" air power led to his court-martial in 1925 and his resignation from the Army the next year.

In his last decade, Mitchell was a lonely man. He died in 1936. Unfortunately, he didn't live to see his dreams realized.

A dashing figure, Billy was often at Langley Field during his years in the Army. In 1920, when aviation leaders dedicated the new Langley Memorial Aeronautical Laboratory—predecessor of today's National Aeronautics and Space Administration—Mitchell led a 25-plane formation over Langley in celebration.

Throughout his life, Mitchell made himself a nuisance in promoting air power. Tall, thin and handsome, he was in demand as a speaker and wrote two books, *Winged Defense,* and *Skyways.* He urged the need for strategic bombing, airborne infantry units and polar air routes. His proposals created strong division even after his ship bombardment experiments off the Capes.

Airplanes were not the only flying machines tested at Langley Field in Billy Mitchell's day. Langley also became a center for Army lighter-than-air experiments with balloons and dirigibles. Germany's Graf zeppelin and Italy's airship *Roma* both excited attention in those years, and the United States in 1921 bought the *Roma* from Italy and brought her to Langley. She was tested to determine her feasibility for transport or warfare.

But technical problems beset the huge hydrogen-filled airship from the start. After three troubled trial flights, the *Roma* left Langley February 21, 1922, to fly over Hampton, Newport News and Norfolk. While approaching the Army Base at Norfolk, the gas bag began to collapse and the *Roma* plunged to the ground.

Striking power lines, the dirigible's hydrogen ignited and turned the huge ship to flames. Crewmen jumped to earth, most of them being killed by the impact. The crash killed 34, but 11 men escaped.

The disaster killed the Army's interest in lighter-than-air vehicles but the Navy continued dirigible experiments for several years.

Mitchell's campaign for an Air Force co-equal with the Army and Navy was realized in 1947, when Congress created one from the former Army Air Corps. Langley Field became one of its most important bases, today headquarters of the Air Combat Command.

Author's photo

Glider atop upper wing was towed by Curtiss Jenny for early air combat training target.

34. *A Hard Trip to Williamsburg*

TRAVEL WAS SLOW and laborious in Model T days in Tidewater. A visit from Deltaville in Middlesex County to Williamsburg, 50 miles away, required driving at 20 miles per hour over dirt roads and crossing both the Piankitank and York rivers by ferry boats.

An account of an arduous "pleasure" trip was published recently by Randolph Norton in the Middlesex County weekly paper. Norton was 16 and proudly drove his parents and two Baltimore guests to the Peninsula to see unrestored Williamsburg in the early 1920s.

They set out early one morning in "dog days," in August, he wrote, when "crops were laid by, and the oyster season was in the offing. Papa and Mama just had to see Williamsburg for the first time." Norton wrote. A lot of Virginians felt the same way.

At the Piankitank River—then without a bridge—they were ferried across by "a scow-type ferry, pulled and pushed by a small workboat with a two-cycle, one-cylinder motor." To board the ferry, "you drove down to the river's edge and blew the horn for the ferry operator to come across from Mathews, where he lived."

Gloucester's roads were unmarked by route signs, but Norton's sea-going father guided them by dead reckoning. "Threading the way wasn't much of a problem for Papa," he wrote, "the navigator who always had a compass in his head."

"I thought the ferry boat between Gloucester Point and Yorktown was about the biggest thing on water," Norton wrote of the boats, then operated by Captain William Ashe, that traveled from Gloucester Point to Yorktown. They docked in Yorktown at the foot of Ballard Street, adjoining

Daily Press

To reach Williamsburg in 1920s, many visitors crossed York on early ferry Cornwallis.

106

Colonial Williamsburg

Williamsburg's best hotel before Rockefeller was Colonial Inn on Duke of Gloucester Street.

the Monument Lodge, near the later site of the Duke of York Motel.

Norton started driving from Yorktown to Williamsburg but encountered a wide mudhole that made the road impassable. "But an enterprising farmer with two of the biggest, blackest mules you ever saw was there to make a buck," Norton remembers. "He hitched us behind his team and collected his fee on the town side of the mud."

Reaching Williamsburg in the afternoon, Norton's family checked into "an old hotel right out of vintage Charles Dickens." It could have been the Colonial Inn, then on Duke of Gloucester Street, on the present site of Chowning's Tavern. The visitors were delighted. "The whole town was a Norman Rockwell picture postcard. No pavement, no stoplights, no fast foods, no trouble parking anywhere."

The next day the travelers "visited all the old places, which it seems had been left untouched since George Washington, Patrick Henry, and the Lees left it for Richmond." At Eastern State Hospital, then called the "Insane Asylum," they visit-

College Corner in the 1920s was a student hangout, with tearoom and bus stop behind it.

Colonial Williamsburg

ed "a rather smart native of Deltaville committed there." Then it was on to see Bruton Parish Church and the site of the colonial Capitol. They returned home that afternoon by way of West Point and Saluda, nervously crossing the C&O railroad tracks along the way. "We arrived home the second evening of our safari," Norton recalls, "without having to use the tire-patching tube or the pump kept under the front seat." (Flat tires were frequent then.)

Norton remembers that the Model T had no door on the driver's side. "For you who never knew the Model T Ford, before the day of self-starters and storage batteries," he said, "we did have a horn that blew when you squeezed the rubber bulb, but that was mainly to get the chickens off the road or to warn a farmer to hold a tighter rein on his horse. You didn't need a driver's license, or insurance, or a credit card, or seat belts, or a car trunk."

Another view of pre-Rockefeller Williamsburg comes from the printed program of a July 4 patriotic pageant, held in front of the College of William and Mary in 1921. Mrs. J.M. Haughwout, who owned the Bull's Head Tavern, was chairman of the celebration. Heading up the program were librarian Earl Gregg Swem and historian John Lesslie Hall of the College of William and Mary.

The costumed pageant was in five acts, each performed to a narrative that was read to the crowd. Professor T.J. Blocker performed as Governor Fauquier, suitably bewigged. Acting as members of the Virginia Council were such leading townsmen as law professor Oscar Shewmake, sawmill owner W.A. Bozarth, innkeeper J.B.C. Spencer, agricultural researcher Preston Cocke, realty agent Archie Brooks, and Professor Donald Davis.

Others in the cast included the Reverend Ruffin Jones of Bruton Parish Church, attorney Thomas Geddy, Dean Kremer Hoke of the college, banker Fred Savage and college business manager C.J. Duke. As the climax of the afternoon's entertainment, a group of younger Williamsburgers performed the minuet, dressed in colonial costume.

All of the group are now dead, but I recognized familiar names. One was Van Garrett Jr., son of the college's science professor, who became an Episcopal minister. Another was Bathurst Dangerfield Peachy, who later became James City County's Commonwealth's attorney.

Among women dancers were Muriel Bozarth, who later married "Bat" Peachy; Lucille Foster; Mary Ware Galt, who married V. Lee Kirby; and others whom the program describes as "beaux and belles."

The program explains that the scenes are supposed to be taking place in the old Capitol. "On account of the expense, all members of the House of Burgesses could not be represented."

That was Williamsburg before it became sophisticated.

35. *The Navy's First Carrier*

A DOZEN MEN who survived two Pacific ship sinkings in two days in World War II were honored in 1983 at a memorable ship's reunion on Mercury Boulevard in Newport News.

They were members of the crew of the USS *Langley*—the Navy's first converted aircraft carrier—which was sunk by the Japanese in February 1942 in the Indian Ocean. Rescued by the Navy oiler *Pecos,* crew members came under attack again by Japanese planes a day later. And most of those who survived the two ordeals were lost when the *Pecos* was finally sunk near Java in the Indian Ocean.

Only a third of the crewmen of the *Langley* and *Pecos* escaped alive from the final disaster, which killed about 700 men. The Naval Institute at Annapolis calls it "one of the most monumentally stupid" operations of the war, resulting from "bureaucratic bungling."

The *Langley's* first three years as an aircraft carrier were spent in Hampton Roads, where Navy flyers made the first shipboard takeoffs and landings in Navy history. That was from 1922 to 1925, after the *Langley* had been converted and commissioned as a carrier at Norfolk Navy Shipyard in Portsmouth.

Old salts like to reminisce about "The Covered Wagon" as they called the ungainly ship. "There was never a ship more beloved by her crew," says Earl Gainer, a retired Navy chief petty officer in Newport News, who was long president of the Covered Wagon Association. Many survivors at the reunion talked about the ordeal.

The fame of the Navy's first carrier has been partly obscured by the second *Langley,* commissioned at Camden, New Jersey, in 1943 and active during World War II. But Gainer and his ex-shipmates are more interested in the old Navy coal ship, which was rebuilt with the Navy's first flight deck in 1922 at Norfolk. Later on, the *Langley* was converted again, that time into a seaplane tender.

"She wasn't a pretty ship, but she was a good one" says Gainer. "And few ships have made as much history as she did," he adds, pointing to her early experiments with planes.

One naval historian of World War II has called the Navy's assignment of the *Langley* to deliver 32 P-40 fighter planes to the Allies in the Pacific "a costly mistake in which nearly 800 men and three United States navy ships were lost." It was indeed a sad story.

Daily Press photo by Christopher Cheyne

U.S. Navy fleet, shown here at Old Point in 1909, had no aircraft carrier until 1922.

Known in the Navy as CV-1, the *Langley* began life in the pre-air age as a Navy coal ship, the USS *Jupiter*. Built at Mare Island, California, in 1913, she served as a coal ship in World War I until chosen by the Navy for conversion as the Navy's first carrier. In 1937 she was changed into a seaplane tender, and in this role served three months against the Japanese before being sunk.

The *Langley* was with the Navy's Asiatic fleet in the Philippines in 1941 when Japan bombed Pearl Harbor on December 7. Early crewmen described her as homely, clumsy, and slow. She could steam only 16 miles an hour.

In October of 1922 the *Langley* accomplished the first carrier-deck launching on the York near Yorktown. "The nettings along both edges of the flight deck were filled with people," writes one observer. "More excited spectators were lined up on the nearby shores of the York River."

Later that month, Navy Lieutenant Commander Godfrey Chevalier landed the first plane on an American carrier at sea when he brought his plane onto the *Langley's* deck near Cape Henry in a 30-knot wind. The next month the *Langley* catapulted a seaplane into the air from her deck—the first such launching from an American carrier in history.

"The *Langley* started the serious business of developing a new form of naval warfare," writes one historian. "Because the British were so secretive about their own carrier effort, the Americans had to develop carrier aviation from scratch."

And to think that much of this happened in Hampton Roads.

The *Langley* was anchored in Manila Bay on December 8, 1941, when the Japanese attacked the Philippines, simultaneous with their attacks on Pearl Harbor and Malaya. However, the *Langley* escaped damage. Two months later she was dispatched by the Joint Allied command of the Southwest Pacific to transport American fighter planes from Australia to Java.

That was where the Navy made its most horrendous mistake of the war, critics say. It was while the ship undertook this mission near Java on February 28, 1942, that the *Langley* was fatally hit by the Japanese. It was a "monumentally stupid" assignment, representing "political expediency and bad bureaucratic bungling."

After Jap bombs hit the slow-moving ship, she began to list and caught fire. The captain gave orders to abandon ship, and men in life jackets plunged into the ocean. Two accompanying destroyers, USS *Edsall* and USS *Whipple*, picked up survivors. Few of the *Langley's* 500-man crew were missing at that point.

Two destroyers transferred the *Langley's* men to the Navy oil tanker *Pecos,* which the Japanese attacked almost immediately. After a bitter attack from four nearby Japanese carriers, the *Pecos* began to burn and sink. Her captain ordered her abandoned.

The last radio message by the *Pecos,* sent out at 3:30 P.M. on March 1, 1942, said "sinking rapidly and the Japs are coming back to give us another dose of what the U.S. is going to give back in larger quantities." Then the oiler sank.

After that, Japanese cruisers and destroyers steamed up and attacked the *Edsall,* which had rescued the *Pecos's* survivors. Soon she too was sunk, together with her crew and 32 Army passengers. Of three ships which had sailed with the *Langley,* only the destroyer *Whipple* remained afloat.

After floating four hours in the sea, survivors of *Langley* and *Pecos* were spotted about 7 p.m. by the *Whipple,* which rescued 233. It estimated that another 450 men were unrescued and perished without trace. After the *Whipple* reached Fremantle, Australia, the survivors transferred to the USS *Mount Vernon* and went back to the United States.

Honoring the *Langley,* a second carrier was commissioned with that name at New York Shipyard in 1943. She served throughout the war and was later used by the French till returned to the United States and scrapped.

"She was a good ship," says one Covered Wagon survivor, "but she didn't make history like the first *Langley.*"

That would be hard to do.

First U.S. carrier Langley *was converted at Norfolk Navy Yard in 1922 from Navy collier.*

Daily Press

36. *The Schneider Cup Races*

DOES ANYBODY besides me remember the 1926 Schneider Cup seaplane races in Hampton Roads? I'd forgotten about them until Martin Gracey of NASA/Langley sent me a copy of Smithsonian *Air and Space* magazine, which contains a fascinating account of the Schneider international seaplane races held in the nascent years of flight.

The Schneider "ended as the symbol of a contest among nations that foreshadowed" World War II declares the magazine.

I remember going with my parents on November 13, 1926, to the Boat Harbor, which was one of three points on Hampton Roads that the six contending Italian and American planes were required to circuit in the race that day. Many people drove to the Boat Harbor to watch the race, parking close to the Hampton Roads ferry dock and the then-recently abandoned Curtiss airfield.

In the 1920s buildup of air power, the race was important. The publication *Aeronautical Chronology* declares: "Due to its historical importance and international aspect, as well as the almost phenomenal speeds achieved, the 1926 race for the Jacques Schneider Trophy may well be regarded as the greatest air race ever held." Those "phenomenal speeds" reached 348 mph, which isn't much now but was great then.

I was 11 in 1926. My parents frequently took my brothers and me on Sundays to Langley Field, which had started 10 years earlier, to see the planes and dirigibles. Across Hampton Roads, the Navy had, since 1917, been building its present naval base. The waterfront there was the starting point of the Schneider races.

Perfect weather attracted some 30,000 spectators, according to *Aeronautical Chronology*. Among spectators were Secretary of the Navy Curtis Wilbur and Assistant Secretary E.P. Warner, along with the Italian ambassador and others.

Seaplanes were popular then. Frenchman Jacques Schneider started an international speed race in 1912 as the counterpart of Gordon Pennett's earlier prize competition for land-based planes.

The United States won the Schneider Cup in 1924 and 1925. If it won again in 1926, it could permanently own the trophy. Alas, that was not to be.

The American winner in 1925 at Baltimore was Army Lieutenant Jimmy Doolittle, who went on to fame in World War II. His Curtiss plane reached a speed of 232 mph—unprecedented in 1925.

112

This R.J. Mitchell seaplane represented United States in 1926 Schneider Cup Race in Hampton Roads.

"But the U.S. government was not prepared to support the rapidly escalating costs of any further development work, leaving the Americans with no new aircraft for 1926," says *Air & Space* magazine. Then Benito Mussolini, the Italian dictator, stepped in. "He saw an opportunity to show the world that nothing was too difficult for a Fascist state," says *Air & Space*. He told Italy's air industry to "win the Schneider trophy at all costs." The Italian engineer, Fiat, developed a racing engine inspired by earlier Curtiss engines.

The French and British meanwhile dropped out, leaving the 1926 race between Italy and the United States. Both nations suffered losses in developing planes and training pilots for the race. The United States lost three aircraft and two pilots in the last weeks before competition. During the preliminary trials in Hampton Roads, one Navy flyer was killed and another barely escaped when his plane capsized in choppy water.

Of the six seaplanes which crossed the starting line at Norfolk's Naval Operating Base, only four finished. One Italian plane was forced down by a broken oil line, while an American was forced down by lack of gasoline.

Thanks to their new Fiat engines and Macchi plane designs, the Italians won the 1926 cup. They broke four world speed records for seaplanes, beating that set by Doolittle the preceding year at Baltimore. But the United States took second when Lieutenant Frank Schilt of the Marine Corps flew a Curtiss seaplane (the same design of the year before) at a speed of 231 mph.

After the races, Italian pilot Mario de Bernardi sent a telegram from Virginia to Mussolini in Rome: "Your orders to win at all costs have been carried out."

That was the last time the United States raced for the Schneider Trophy, leaving later competitions to the Italians and British.

According to *Air & Space*, "many people felt that an attempt should be made to achieve a third victory. but the manufacturers had had quite enough of experimenting and longed for more

114 *Along Virginia's Golden Shores*

Daily Press

Schneider Cup race for planes in 1926 took off from Newport News Boat Harbor, shown in 1927.

profitable ventures. Neither the Navy nor the Army was prepared to set aside further funds for racing aircraft, thus the United States never again raced for the Schneider Trophy.

Air & Space attributes Great Britain's successful design of its World War II Spitfire to experience in the Schneider races. It concludes that "some of the foundation upon which the Royal Air Force built its victory [in World War II] against the Luftwaffe in the Battle of Britain" was gained in the Schneider races.

Many pioneers of military aviation trained on the Peninsula in those days. General Billy Mitchell learned to fly at the pre-World War I Curtiss Field at the Boat Harbor, while other Army flyers like General Hap Arnold trained at Langley Field after its founding in 1916.

A lot of aviation history has been made on this Peninsula.

37. *The Heyday of Bridge Building*

GRATITUDE, that rare virtue, flowed generously in 1928, when a Newport News civic delegation paid its own way to Boston one hot August weekend to thank William A. Paine and other officials of a Boston underwriting firm for selling the bonds that made possible the four-mile-long James River Bridge to Southside.

On November 17, 1928, the day the bridge was opened, President Calvin Coolidge in Washington pressed the button that lifted the draw span while Governor Harry Byrd spoke to the crowd at the intersection of Warwick Boulevard and the bridge approach in Newport News.

I was there and watched Woodroof Hiden (later Mrs. Wendell Hussey) wield the giant scissors that cut the ribbon. Crossing was free that day, but tolls were charged later until the state took over the bridge and paid off the bonds.

But about that gratitude: Money was getting tight in 1928, a year before the Wall Street crash and the time that $1 million in bonds needed to be sold to pay for the bridge construction.

Fortunately, civic spark plug Philip Hiden of Newport News was able to get Boston financiers to advance the sum. Thereupon, Walter Scott Copeland, editor of *The Times-Herald* and president of the Chamber of Commerce, led a "thank you" mission composed of Peninsula big-wigs to Boston. He and Hiden had conceived the bridge.

I learned all this from a newspaper account written by a former Newport News resident, Susan Macomber, who then lived in Allston, Massachusetts. She also gave her recollections of the 1880s and 1890s in Newport News. She wrote:

> Many years ago when that thriving and enterprising city was in its infancy, having a population of about 800, I lived there, walked its unpaved streets, bathed in the James that laps its pebbly beach, went crabbing from the little pavilion that jutted out into the river belonging to the Warwick [hotel], rode horseback to Old Point, (for it was then the only means of reaching there), danced to the music of the band in the old Hygeia [hotel] ballroom, saw the rich golden sunset cast its flaming rays of purple, yellow, primrose and azure across the seven-mile mouth of the beautiful, rolling James and reveled in the afterglow, for in no other place does the sun set in such splendor—not even in California—as in Virginia.

Miss Macomber went on to recall people in Newport News:

Newport News tycoon Philip W. Hiden led private investors to build James River bridge in 1928.

Newport News newspaperman W. Scott Copeland led goodwill trip to thank bridge investors.

Those were golden days, the happiest in my life, for not only was Newport News rich in her sunsets, moonlight and sunrises, but she numbered among her inhabitants families whose names were famous among the F.F.V. and whose courtesy and culture stood highest in this broad land of ours.

For such names as Braxton, Slaughter, Lee, Gordon, Ficklin, Post, Jones, Massey, Peachey, Cromwell and many others were familiar to us all, and although houses were few and far between then, and money not plentiful, for we were all pioneers, blazing a trail for today, yet Newport News was rich in culture and grace.

Religion played a strong part, too, for there was the little Union Chapel, which on the first Sunday of the month was used by the Baptists, on the second Sunday by the Methodists, the third by the Presbyterians, the fourth by the Episcopalians, and if there was a fifth Sunday, by anyone.

It was hard then to tell to which denomination anyone belonged, for we all attended every Sunday.

These families were the pioneers of Newport News, and although they basked and nearly melted beneath the warm sun, yet their faith in the ultimate growth of the city as planned and laid out by the Old Dominion Land Company, under Mr. C.P. Orcutt, never wavered.

Miss Macomber paid tribute to Colonel Carter Braxton, a Newport News pioneer who served in the Confederacy, engineered the C&O right of way from Lee Hall to Newport News in the 1870s, and supervised excavations for the shipyard in the 1890s.

She added, "I can see Colonel Braxton, strong of feature, kindly of face, broad-shouldered, courteous—for he was of the old school—firm in his conviction that the little sand plain of a city would one day become a great and powerful one, which would be to Virginia one of her proudest possessions."

She concluded her paean: "It is 40 years since I first went to Newport News, to make my home (I was but 15 then), ... but to me, New England-born, there never was a fairer, more beautiful place, for my heart's in Virginia."

The most exciting event of my childhood in Newport News was the opening of the bridge on

November 17, 1928. It was especially meaningful to my family because it opened an automobile route to Smithfield, the town from which my parents had moved to Newport News in 1918. It replaced a slow boat trip.

The multimillion-dollar highway bridge was news all over the country, for then it was the longest in the nation—nearly five miles—with a lift tall enough to clear the tallest ships. President Calvin Coolidge pressed an electric button in the White House that afternoon to lower the upraised lift span and permit the first ceremonial limousines to cross it. "Silent Cal" didn't say a word, but that was all right with spectators in Newport News.

Governor Harry Byrd came from Richmond to speak at the ceremonies on the bridge approachway on Warwick Boulevard. But the big attraction for me—then a 13-year-old—was the ceremonial cutting of the ribbon by "Miss Virginia," who wielded a 4-foot-long pair of scissors.

Recalling the event today, I feel sorry for the private investors who put up the millions to build the bridge, for 11 months after the bridge opened, the stock market crashed and the value of the bonds immediately plummeted. Eventually, though, the state of Virginia bought up the bonds and made the bridge part of the state highway system.

The bridge's chief investor was former Newport News Mayor Philip W. Hiden. He had made a lot of money during World War I as a grain broker, providing feed for livestock being shipped to Europe. After the war, he bought the Army's warehouses along Warwick Boulevard and used them for tobacco storage for his Hiden Storage and Forwarding Company.

He had been chosen Newport New's mayor in 1921 when the city adopted the mayor, council and city manager plan of government.

According to Copeland's daughter, Mrs. Fillmore Norfleet of Charlottesville, the two men—neighbors living on Huntington Avenue—cogitated long and often about what they could do for Newport News. Their idea of the bridge, she told me, "evolved from their wish to open up to the produce farmers of Southside the larger markets of the North."

The state then let private investors operate highway bridges and ferries, so Hiden and

Five-mile long James River Bridge in 1928 began wave of bridge-building to link Tidewater.

Daily Press

Copeland developed their plan as a private enterprise and got wealthy men in Tidewater and New England to invest in it. They chose Turner Construction Company of New York to build the bridge and the investment firm of Paine Webber & Company in New York to finance it.

In 1926, after the bonds had been bought up, Copeland persuaded the Virginia Chamber of Commerce to send a delegation of businessmen to Boston to thank New England investors for the confidence.

Writes Elizabeth Norfleet: "The trip was my father's idea. As president of the Virginia Press Association and the Newport News Chamber of Commerce he arranged the trip as a sightseeing venture . . . to express the thanks of Newport News and Virginia citizens for its trust."

The James River Bridge opening started with a lunch at the Hotel Warwick for Byrd and other officials. After lunch, the stylish Richmond Blues, an elite military unit that had fought in World War 1, paraded to the bridge site. Then a squadron of nine Langley planes and two dirigibles flew over the bridge. Two vessels representing the Monitor and the Merrimack re-enacted the 1862 Battle of the Ironclads.

Hiden's daughter, Woodroof, wielded the scissors as "Miss Virginia" to cut the bridge ribbon, aided by Copeland's daughter as "Miss Newport News." Gathered around were a dozen other princesses from other Tidewater towns, all dressed to kill and bearing bouquets of roses and ribbons of identification. Copeland had died before the bridge was completed.

The highlight came when "Miss Virginia" cut the ribbon at exactly 4:30. At that moment President Coolidge in the White House pressed the button to lower the lift. In the river a gun was fired and the cruiser USS *Marblehead* turned her searchlights on the lift span. The Richmond Blues band played "The Star-Spangled Banner," and everybody's blood tingled.

The day's program lists events from 7 A.M. to 6:15 P.M., when the governor's train took him and the Richmond Blues back to Richmond.

After the ribbon-cutting, most of the crowd rushed to the banks of the James, where Windward Towers now stands, and watched the Battle of the Ironclads refought, this time with fireworks. After the performance of Byrd, Silent Cal and the "princesses," it was an anticlimax. The bridge, though, lived up to all of Hiden's and Copeland's expectations.

Unfortunately, the bridge fared poorly as a revenue producer in its early years, hurt by the Depression, but bridge bondholders were paid off later when the Commonwealth of Virginia bought and operated it. It was a godsend to shipyard commuters in World War II, and it has had to be rebuilt in recent years to handle increasingly heavy traffic.

Happily, part of the original bridge adjoining Newport News' Huntington Park was left as a fishermen's pier. It too is widely used.

Bathing beaches and pleasure casino were features of early Newport News, seen here at 25th Street.

38. *Wild Beaches of Yesteryear*

IF YOU WANT to see how the Virginia Peninsula has built up since World War II, just look at its waterfront. When I grew up in Newport News, children could swim in many places. Not today. In the 1930s the Peninsula offered free bathing beaches from Jamestown on the James all the way around Newport News and Hampton and up to Yorktown. Now most Peninsula beaches are restricted.

In the laissez-faire 1920s, the James River north of the shipyard was a summer haven for North Enders. We could keep boats and swim anywhere from what was the northern boundary of the shipyard at 53rd Street all the way up to what we called "Watts' Creek"—it was really Waters' Creek—now dammed to create the Mariners' Museum's Lake Maury.

I remember Jim Walker's boat-rental pier about 54th Street and Captain Seay's at 58th. Another rental pier—Red Crossley's, I think—stood about where the Windward Towers now loom at the James River Bridge. All that began to change in 1928 when the bridge was built. Then came the Mariners' Museum in 1931, and in World War II came the shipyard's expansion, the biggest change of all.

So far as I remember, downtowners made little use of the narrow beach along the Casino, from 25th Street to the shipyard. Before World War II the shoreline was occupied by Pier A at 25th Street and the Warwick Machine Company repair pier a few blocks to the north.

Collis Huntington's original Warwick Hotel, built in the 1880s, had planned to make use of the Casino shore, for an early advertising illustration shows the shore with a bathhouse and swimmers. Though the Casino grounds were used for games and gatherings, I don't remember seeing anyone swimming there.

Hampton's equivalent of North End was the Boulevard. In its early days the shoreline was farther out than today, with a pleasant sand beach for swimming. Some riparian rights owners had docks and kept boats. Some had duck blinds. Few of either survive, however.

People who lived on the Boulevard used to boast of the soft-crabbing, fishing, and duck hunting they enjoyed in the 1920s and early '30s. Then along came the 1933 hurricane. It swept away much of the beach and ate deeply into Chesapeake Avenue, which follows the Boulevard shoreline. The area hasn't been the same since.

Until then, the Newport News-Hampton trolley had followed the shoreline between the two

119

Knees of ancient cypresses line creeks and marshes surrounding Jamestown on James River.

cities, but its right-of-way was largely destroyed by the hurricane. When rebuilt, the trackage was wisely moved inland. It didn't make for a pretty trolley ride, but it reduced Boulevard traffic.

In the 1920s and '30s the Peninsula had commercial beaches at Buckroe, Grandview, and at Bay Shore, but all have been redeveloped. When the last owners of Buckroe's amusement park, the Stieffen family, sold out, the area lost what remained of its original resort character. It wasn't anyone's fault; it's just that tastes change.

Goodwin's Island, a low-lying York River area close to Marlbank, once offered possibilities as a recreation beach, but it has been given by its last owners to the College of William and Mary. Stanley Abbott, who was in the 1950s a farseeing superintendent of Colonial National Historical Park, urged that Virginia buy Goodwin's Island as a swimming beach. Then, he pointed out, the National Park Service could consider ending swimming in Yorktown.

However, instead of buying Goodwin's Island, the Virginia Parks and Recreation Division bought land at Croaker and created York River State Park west of Williamsburg. Unfortunately, the park's river front has a shallow bot-

Virginia Gazette

Countless creeks and marshes grow the plants and sea life that enrich Chesapeake Bay system.

tom, unsuited for swimming. So bathers continue to flock instead to Yorktown and Gloucester Point.

It's regrettable that so much of York County's beautiful waterfront is lined by large federal holdings, which must deny the public access to the river. The federal occupants are the Coast Guard Station, Naval Weapons Station, Cheatham Annex, and Camp Peary. True, the Colonial National Historical Park controls some of the waterfront, but it permits swimming only at Yorktown.

Someday, I hope York County can obtain more beach property and create another Peninsula recreation area. If the historic wharf area of Yorktown is redeveloped, as is now being discussed, beach bathing there will be further crowded.

Peninsula beaches should offer recreation to the public, no matter how built-up this area is becoming. As it is, a few landowners, military bases, and corporations are in position to hog them all.

39. *Langley's Daring Young Men*

I WILL NEVER FORGET a dinner I attended in February 1939 with a group of Army Air Corps officers at Langley Field. One of them, Colonel Walter Weaver, predicted that Adolf Hitler would engulf Europe in war within 60 days.

I was a reporter, trained to be skeptical, but I soon found that the colonel was right. Within a month Der Fuhrer seized Bohemia and Moravia, and World War II erupted. In no time at all I was off to war myself.

The prewar years were exciting on the Peninsula. Uncle Sam was building up the Army and Navy, and the Newport News shipyard was going full steam. Military bases and industries worked round the clock.

Langley Field was exciting in those days because of the emerging potential of aviation in warfare. Air Corps officers like Hap Arnold, Carl Spaatz, Bob Stratemeyer, Ira Eaker, Frank Andrews and Arnold Krogstad were showing what airplanes could do. All would become famous in the war.

I remember a mission flown from Langley Field to South America by a force of Flying Fortresses led by Colonel Robert Old. It was billed as a "good-will mission" to Brazil, Argentina and Colombia, but actually it was to impress, the world with America's might.

"Fly boys" at Langley Field were thought by Peninsula girls in those days to have more than their share of pizazz. Beirne Lay, who married a Hampton girl named Ludwell Lee, was an example. Besides flying, he wrote *I Wanted Wings* which became a hit movie. And Langley's Flying Fortresses and their crews took part in MGM's successful "Test Pilot" in 1938, with Spencer Tracy, Myrna Loy and Clark Gable. Scenes were filmed at Langley.

A lot was going on, too, at the NACA—the National Advisory Committee for Aeronautics—also quartered at Langley Field. (It was the predecessor of the NASA.) There a lot of daring young men were testing new aircraft. We Peninsula boys resented them because they dated Hampton and Newport News girls. Most had zippy roadsters and wore beards, which we Peninsula high schoolers were unaccustomed to.

Many of them came from California, where the Old Testament look was stylish.

One of the "NACA nuts," as they called themselves, was Eastman Jacobs, an interesting scientist who has now retired on the West Coast. Other NACA pioneers now live on the Peninsula.

Aerial view shows Curtiss Airfield at Newport News Boat Harbor in 1948, Langley's predecessor.

Langley Field in the 1930s also had experimental dirigibles, which were berthed in a big hangar apart from the airplanes. All the hangars smelled of banana oil, which my brothers and I used in making balsa models of airplanes. I still associate banana oil with Langley.

A great outburst of housing went on in Newport News and Hampton then to accommodate the buildup of military personnel and shipyard workers. The first project was Ferguson Park, built near the James River Bridge. Then came Stuart Gardens, Copeland Park and Newsome Park.

Fort Eustis revived in the war as a Selective Service training center, and a new Navy receiving station was built near the James River Bridge entrance.

When America entered the war after Japan's attack on Pearl Harbor, most of my generation went off to fight. Many of the military officers who had been stationed at Peninsula bases became famous.

Chief among these was Dwight Eisenhower, who had served at Fort Monroe as a lieutenant colonel. Other Fort Monroe alumni who were given high commands in the war were General Courtney Hodges and General Joseph T. McNamey.

From Langley Field, my old friend and news source, Colonel Walter Weaver, became a three-star general, commanding the Army Air Technical Training Command, which prepared soldiers to repair and service airplanes.

At the shipyard, old hands remembered a slim young officer named Raymond Ames Spruance, who had served his first post-Annapolis duty as a naval shipbuilder in Newport News. He became one of the great admirals.

Much of what went on in Newport News during World War II was shrouded in secrecy. The Navy kept secret all data on warships under construction or repair. And the Hampton Roads Port of Embarkation did its best to send its transports loaded with GIs out into the Atlantic Ocean without letting anybody know. That's because German U-boats lurked beneath the sea lanes, waiting to torpedo any vessel leaving or entering the capes.

A submarine net was strung across the main Hampton Roads channel to enmesh any enemy U-boat trying to enter. And U. S. Navy convoys left port under cover of night to reduce the danger of enemy detection. I sailed for the Sicilian campaign just before dawn.

When I came back to Newport News after four years as a Navy officer, I found everything bigger and more crowded. Overnight, the shipyard, Langley and Fort Eustis had grown immense. Now, many years later, the Cold War has ended and Peninsula defenses are shrinking.

Author's collection

Italian-built dirigible Roma *came to Langley in 1922 but crashed on flight to Norfolk.*

40. *When Prostitutes Flourished*

REPORTS of Heidi Fleiss and her entrepreneurial enterprise in Hollywood suggest that pretty young girls are still willing to do almost anything for a shot at getting in the movies. High-priced prostitution isn't hard to find in the Never-Never Land of the movie stars.

But, however popular they may be in California, sporting houses have disappeared from most Virginia localities. The old days of licensed Virginia bawdy houses have gone. In Newport News, the temples of Venus that once flourished on downtown streets have been torn down in an orgy of urban rehabilitation.

Time was when Newport News and Hampton, along with Norfolk, Portsmouth, Alexandria, and other Virginia towns had bawdy houses, whose prostitutes underwent weekly health checkups for venereal disease. Then World War II came along, and the Army and Navy put such establishments off-limits to protect our boys in uniform. Since that war, prostitution in Virginia has become less visible.

The best-known Newport News bordellos flourished between the two World Wars on 18th Street, where stood the houses of Lulu and Kate. They catered to lonely seamen and sailors in the days when Newport News was a major port. Later, many prostitutes moved to Warwick Avenue, now called Terminal Boulevard.

Downtown residents in those days enjoyed the weekly parade of prostitutes as they walked to the Newport News city clinic to get their checkup. According to the late Sinclair Phillips, who had his law office on 25th Street, the women would dress in flashy clothes and high-heeled shoes. They smiled and waved to onlookers, obviously unashamed of themselves.

During both World Wars, federal law banned prostitution within five miles of naval and military installations. Some madams accordingly moved their places of business outside the restricted area.

Phoebus was celebrated for its many saloons and houses of prostitution. They were patronized in part by war veterans domiciled at what is now the Kecoughtan Veterans' Facility at Old Point. In those days Phoebus was known widely, along with Newport News, as a sort of oasis for randy sailors of all nationalities.

Virginia's best-known prostitutes were the celebrated Louise and Bernice, who operated well-run establishments in Lynchburg, in the midst of such male strongholds as the University of Virginia, VPI, Washington and Lee, VMI and Hampden-Sydney. One University of Virginia boxing coach of the pre-World War II era promised his team a night's outing at Bernice's at his expense after boxing season if they would keep their training pledge during the season.

Another celebrated students' sporting house was operated in Charlottesville before World War II. In those days, organized prostitution was grudgingly accepted by society as an alternative to rape and seduction.

St. Augustine is quoted as having written: "Remove prostitution from human affairs, and you will pollute all things with lust." And St. Thomas Aquinas added, "Take away prostitutes from the world, and you will fill it with sodomy."

Richmond's most celebrated bordello of the 1930s was run by one Hortense Blair, who claimed to be related to the city's Blair family, which settled in Richmond in Colonial times. Her bordello was over the Richmond Willow Works on Broad Street in an area once dense with saloons.

Probaby the most unusual Virginia bordellos were the "assignation houseboats" on the Potomac River at Alexandria in the 1920s and 1930s. Historians have recently identified the remains of one of more than 1,000 "arks" which accommodated prostitutes and their customers on the Virginia shore between Little Falls in Arlington and Prince William County. Several hundred other arks operated in the District of Columbia and in Maryland.

According to the Virginia Canals and Navigations Society, "Small floating houses of prostitution, most of them painted red or blue (the more high-class boats usually were white with blue roofs and shutters) lined the shores and clustered around gambling casino boats. They flourished because Virginia had no jurisdiction over the

Brothels and saloons flourished in Phoebus to serve sailors and inmates of Soldiers' Home.

Daily Press

Floating brothels like the Dream flourished on the Potomac at Alexandria until World War II.

river and because Maryland and the District ignored them."

According to Alexandria historian Frederick Tilp, "the best-known ark, and the only two-story, four-woman floating brothel on the river, was Madame Rose's 'Dream' boat." It hit the front pages in 1905 when it lost its moorings in a storm and floated down river until fishermen rescued Madam Rose and her girls and customers and towed the Dream to the Maryland shore.

The arks began to thin out when the George Washington Memorial Park was built between Arlington and Mount Vernon in the 1930s. After a brief revival during World War II, the arks disappeared.

The Mariners' Museum has a photograph of Madame Rose's Dream, complete with hanging baskets and flower boxes along its decks. Maybe a look at it would give California's flesh-peddlers some fresh ideas.

41. *Highways Replace Seaways*

ROADS WERE FEW on this Peninsula —and everywhere else in America— until automobiles arrived in 1900 to open up the Age of Travel. More than any other invention, the auto has revolutionized the world. Henry Ford's product in my lifetime has created a new lifestyle—not altogether desirable. It has also put most steamships and trains out of business. Highway traffic grows about four percent annually. That means it nearly doubles every 12 years. Good grief!

The first road built in English America was at Jamestown in 1607 when the Greate Road to the West was blazed across that peninsula's isthmus to Glasshouse Point. Over the years it was extended through the woods of James City to Greenspring, where Governor Sir William Berkeley built the first mansion in America. At Greenspring the Greate Roade divided, one branch going east to Middle Plantation (later Wiliamsburg) an the other west along the James River to the present Richmond.

Today that plantation road is Virginia's picturesque Route 5, called the John Tyler Highway in honor of one of the two presidents born in Charles City County. Loggers and developers threaten the historic road, but driving over it is still pleasurable, especially when the leaves are turning.

Building roads was slow in Virginia's first years, when settlers could travel more easily by rowboat or sailboat over Tidewater's countless creeks and rivers. But horses were soon imported from England—the first in 1611—and "horse paths" and "cart paths' were cut through pine woods. At first each landowner cleared his own

Two Hampton Roads bridge tunnels offer speedy access to Virginia's major ports and cities.

Norfolk Convention and Visitors Bureau

road, but eventually counties began to pay farmers to improve horse paths with sand, marl and gravel during the winter when they weren't busy. Today the Virginia Department of Transportation—VDOT—keeps up most Virginia roads except for city streets and private roads.

Maps of the Peninsula before the 1900s show few roads outside Hampton, Yorktown and Williamsburg. Dirt cart paths connected Williamsburg, Hampton, and Newport News Point, linking the courthouse seats of Elizabeth City, Warwick, York and James City. Another winding road linked Newport News Point and Hampton, predecessor of today's Kecoughtan Road. Rowed or sailed ferries were common in early Tidewater, for bridges came slowly—mostly in this century. In his useful *Tobacco Coast*, published by the Mariners' Museum, Pierce Middleton lists the many ferries licensed by the General Assembly in Colonial years. Travelers had to ford or swim narrow creeks, and wagons had to detour around deep ones.

An early settler named Tyndall (Gloucester Point was first named for him) made charts and maps of early Tidewater, but they were imprecise. The first map-makers to depict the Peninsula adequately were Revolutionary War military engineers who mapped the area before or during Cornwallis' siege of Yorktown. English and French engineers left us the first detailed maps of our area, including the so-called "Frenchman's Map" of Williamsburg in 1782. It's thought to have been drawn for their six-month-long stay in Williamsburg after Cornwallis surrendered in 1781.

The Peninsula's face hadn't changed much when the Civil War struck 81 years later. General George B. McClellan, who led the Union invasion of the Peninsula in 1862, complained about having few good maps. Fortunately, for the Con-

Monitor-Merrimac bridge-tunnel links Newport News, in distance, with Suffolk and Southside.

Daily Press

NASA recognized Hampton Roads' importance in assigning first Mercury astronauts to Langley.

federates, some Peninsula soldiers in the gray-clad army knew the area.

McClellan complained the loudest when heavy rains inundated the Peninsula in the spring of 1862 and turned New Kent Stage Road (running between Williamsburg and Richmond) into a sea of mud. McClellan's deep wagon tracks furrowed the land for years afterward. And then Henry Ford's Model T began to revolutionize America.

Virginia met the need for hard-surfaced roads by creating its first highway department in Richmond, with Williamsburg's George Preston Coleman as its head. One of the first hard-surfaced roads built on the Peninsula was from Williamsburg to Jamestown in 1907 to enable autoists to see America's first permanent English settlement on its 300th anniversary. Today the Coleman Bridge honors him.

When World War I threatened, the Army in 1917 laid down the Peninsula's first hard-surfaced highway, connecting Old Point and Richmond. Part of this is now Route 60. Its purpose was to permit quick egress from Fort Monroe in case of naval attack. Fortunately for the Peninsula, the road ran through Hampton to Newport News over Kecoughtan Road and thence to Williamsburg, where it followed the main Peninsula road up Duke of Gloucester Street to Richmond.

World War II and its aftermath brought the first federal and state program to link the Peninsula with Norfolk, the Eastern Shore and Gloucester. A new Military Highway (now Mercury Boulevard) linked Old Point with the James River Bridge, and the Chesapeake and Hampton Roads bridge-tunnels were constructed. The crowning achievement was the interstate highway system, which now girdles Hampton Roads and speeds traffic in all directions.

42. *The Decline of Oystering*

MY FIRST BEAT as a reporter for the Newport News papers after I graduated from college in 1937 was the Hampton Roads waterfront. Those were the years of the romantic ballad "I Cover the Waterfront," and I thought of it as I hustled with my notepad from the newspaper office on 25th Street down to the C&O piers on the James River, then bustling with ships discharging bauxite, rubber, coffee, and bananas and loading tobacco, cattle and lots of coal.

I miss that earthy bustle when I visit lower Newport News now.

Ships of every nation called there then, and seamen lit up the dock area with nightly revels that sometimes landed them in jail. Prohibition quieted things eventually.

Part of my beat was the Virginia Commission of Fisheries office at 24th Street and West Avenue, where a pious Eastern Shoreman named Walter Mapp tried to save Virginia's fisheries with a small fleet of police boats. Oysters were numerous and profitable, and G. Walter had his hands full to avert hostilities between rival Virginia and Maryland "arstermen" or "sea Ayrabs," as the papers called them.

Those were the days of gun-slinging Chesa-

VIMS photo by William DuPaul

A tonger brings up seed oysters to be hauled by barge and planted to provide more oysters.

Daily Press

Dying breed: oysterman demonstrates old-fashioned oyster tongs on James River tributary.

peake "oyster wars", and the frequent violence was front-page news. Alas, today the decline of the oyster industry has nearly ended oystering and its wars. As biologists had predicted, years of over dredging have reduced supplies of the "luscious bivalve," and in the past five years the spread of oyster diseases has nearly finished them.

Mapp's fisheries commission strove hard to bring peace; he was an earnest and peaceful man. He was abetted by the commission's able lawyer, B. Drummond Ayres, who also came from the Eastern Shore.

The oyster wars tumbled on for 100 years, a tragic era. Watermen are a tough, resentful lot, and they don't like government "meddling." For years after the Civil War they plied their rough trade with few controls by Virginia and Maryland, who share the bay's fisheries under an agreement signed in 1785. But when over-aggressive oystering in the 1870s threatened the oyster supply, both states began imposing laws to reduce the oyster season, to forbid the taking of small oysters and to control oyster "drudging," as the watermen called it.

Despite the so-called Potomac Compact of 1785, bad blood was inevitable between watermen of the two states. For one thing, Maryland had earlier harsher controls, which upset Maryland watermen. Virginia followed a more laissez-faire policy for awhile and then in 1875 created a Commission of Fisheries, to be headquartered in Newport News. In 1968 the commission was succeeded by the Marine Resources Commission, still in downtown Newport News. Today its employees are scattered over Tidewater, roughly half in Newport News and others as sea-going fisheries patrolmen. By the time I encountered the Chesapeake oyster wars in 1937, the worst were over.

By that time the two states had stronger laws and more patrolmen to enforce them. Soon to back up conservation efforts would come the Virginia Institute of Marine Science at Gloucester Point, a research arm of The College of William and Mary.

Many gripes have fed the anger of Chesapeake watermen over the years. It's hard for fishermen to know which underwater area belongs to Virginia and which to Maryland. Or which oyster grounds are public, to be used by all licensed watermen, or private, to be dredged only by the dredger who paid rent for it.

To make matters worse, equipment that oystermen were permitted by the two states to use has sometimes differed, adding to the difficulties of enforcement. "Arstering is the only trade in the world that forbids the use of modern equipment," complained a grizzled waterman at one hearing.

In George Walter Mapp's day, fisheries laws were enforced by a small fleet of motorboats. Seaplanes were introduced later.

A tragedy in 1949 that worsened relations between the two states was the shooting of Earl Nelson, a 60-year-old Crisfield waterman, by Virginia fisheries deputy David Acree. Acree had spotted Nelson's Maryland boat crabbing two miles inside the Virginia boundary, landed his seaplane beside Nelson, and ordered him to steer his craft to a Virginia patrol boat. Acree's rifle accidently went off as the two scuffled, and Nelson was fatally injured.

At last in the 1980s the collapse of Chesapeake oystering finally occurred. Parasitical diseases spread over the oyster bottoms of the Chesapeake, brought on by years of light spring rains, which increased the salinity of bay waters at a crucial time in the oyster's lifespan. Fortunately, the Chesapeake's supplies of crabs and of some fish seem to be holding up better despite man's greed.

When I go back to the waterfront today, everything is changed. I hope the Marine Resources Commission can preserve and increase what's left of our once-abundant bay fisheries, but the fish are going fast.

J.S. Darling oyster plant at Hampton deposited oyster-shell pyramid along Hampton Creek.

Author's collection

IV

The Age of Cities and Towns

Daily Press

Hard crabs are steamed in vats, then removed and cooled before pickers remove their meat.

43. *When Fish and Crabs Abounded*

THE POOR CRAB CATCHES in Virginia waters recently remind me of those summers in the 1920s and 1930s when soft crabs were so plentiful in Newport News they sold for five cents apiece. The James River shoreline from 53rd Street northward to Hilton Village was virgin territory then, with a few cypress and wild plum trees scattered along its shore.

Watermen like Jim Walker, Captain Seay, Mr. Kipper, and Red Crossley kept rowboats to rent for bottom fishing at little commercial piers dotting the shore from 53rd Street to the old Camp Hill Hostess House, then a survivor of World War I.

In those days the James was a paradise of seafood. The shoal waters adjoining North End had endless underwater eelgrass, where peeler crabs could hide out from eels and toad fish while they busted out of their hard shell and grew bigger. We boys built wooden box-floats which trailed behind us from a rope when we started out at low tide with our crab net. Today eelgrass has disappeared from the James and most Chesapeake estuaries, nobody knowing exactly why. It's said to be coming back.

On low tide, when the moon was full (the time most crabs shed), a boy in my youth could catch three or four dozen crabs. At five cents apiece, that came only to $2.40, but that was a good day's income in Depression era Newport News. If they were big crabs, you might even get 75 cents a dozen for them.

Those were the years of the croaker, an abundant saltwater fish that grew to three or four

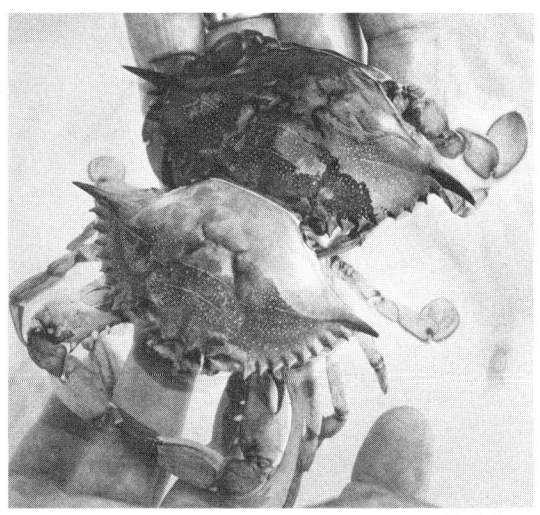

Daily Press

Crabs 'bust' open in life cycle to grow up. Here soft crab emerges from shell.

Skilled crab picker works rapidly to permit fresh seafood to reach worldwide market.

pounds. You'd catch the big ones in the channel near the shipyard or the James River Bridge. Some restaurants sold them as "Norfolk spot" if the spot weren't running.

We also caught a lot of trout, sometimes called weakfish, plus hogfish, dogfish (sand sharks), and those mud toads that some VIMS scientists said were good to eat but that my wife says weren't. We were common "bottom fishermen," disdained now by the sportier blue fishermen and rock fishermen, but we didn't care.

My brothers and I owned a rowboat tied in low water in the James at 59th Street, and we'd catch enough crabs for bait and the row out to the channel to fish on high tide. We caught so many fish sometimes we couldn't give them away. One summer we salted them down, but they weren't half so tasty as those high-smelling herring my father bought in wooden buckets each fall.

Once when were fishing near the Shipyard we got run off by a shipyard tug. The yard was about to send a ship down the launching skids and it needed plenty of free water to catch the sliding hull and haul it back to a construction pier.

As we boys grew bigger we were invited now and then to go on deepwater fishing trips with my father, usually leaving the Boat Harbor. If the weather was mild we'd fish off Hampton Bar, which was famous for its spot fishing, or off Grandview, famous for its gray trout.

Lots of people of only modest means had launches in those days of cheap gasoline. Many were berthed at the Boat Harbor and others on Hampton Creek.

A favorite fishing ground was the deepwater channel off the Newport News coal and general cargo piers. There, at Point Breeze, the James River merges into Hampton Roads, creating a strong current. When the C&O built its Newport News terminals in 1881, it dredged deeply at that point to give plenty of depth for ships to maneuver. Maybe that's why it seemed to attract the biggest fish.

But life in Virginia's rivers changes, and they are no longer the Eden of plenty they once were. Outboard motors became universal in the 1930s, and they speeded up water travel. It suddenly seemed unbearable to have to row out to the channel when you could motor there in a third the time. Everybody bought a one-horsepower Ivor Johnson; now they've grown tremendously in power and speed, afflicting waterways with noise and danger.

In 1928 came the James River Bridge, hastening the buildup of the river's shoreline and forming a boundary for awhile of North End's buildup. Suddenly the sense of unexploited nature was lost. But we continued for awhile to enjoy good fishing, especially around the bridge pillars. Their underwater growth attracted minnows, which in turn lured bigger fish.

Many fishermen enjoy fishing now from the leftover stub of the original James River Bridge, projecting from Huntington Park. This innocent pastime is the birthright of every American, but

Crab pots have revolutionized crabbing, attracting huge catches to baited wire traps.

free fishing sites have dwindled alarmingly. Virginia can learn in this respect from Florida, which builds bridges wide to accommodate its Izaak Waltons.

One of the changes on the James occurred at Waters Creek, once in Warwick County and now in Newport News. Once it was a rustic waterway that flowed into the James next door to Doug Smith's Cedar Lane plantation. People mistakenly called it Watts Creek, just as they perverted Salford's Creek into Salter's and Keith's Creek into Skiffe's.

In 1930 Archer Huntington bought Waters Creek and its surrounding acreage as the site of the Mariners' Museum. No longer could we North Enders paddle up the creek and tease the water moccasins. The creek was dammed to form Lake Maury, to the dismay of muskrats, herons, and beavers galore. But the museum and lake have been a great boon to the Peninsula.

When I think of Virginia's rivers in Depression years, I recall only their pleasures. Let's hope the Chesapeake's waters will remain accessible to the great American public, as they were when I was young.

Captain A.F. Jester of Smithfield operated James River ferries at Jamestown and Chuckatuck in 1920s.

Daily Press

44. *Ferries Still Ply the River*

WHENEVER I cross the Jamestown ferry to Surry County, I'm struck by the contrast between Southside and the rest of Virginia. Those southern counties seem to be a survival of the 19th century, where people still live the rural, slow-paced life of tobacco-planting days. It's like going from today to the world I knew as a boy in the 1930s.

As I make my way from Scotland Wharf past the Rolfe-Warren house and on to Surry Courthouse, I sense a different existence out there in the peanut fields and pine forests. Southsiders are people who march to the beat of a different drum. Many live on land inherited from generations past. They aren't the slaves of time and conformity that the rest of us have to be.

Surry is part of me because my mother and her parents were born there. It may be a small and modest county today, since it lost most of its early acreage to Sussex and Brunswick, but in colonial times it was an important county of plantations and slaveholdings. The Allens of Bacon's Castle and Claremont Manor were then the richest family in Virginia. Their slaves were rented to the Confederacy to build fortifications at Jamestown and other James River promontories to deter Federal ships from going up the James to attack the Confederates in Richmond.

William Short, who was one of Phi Beta Kappa's founders at William and Mary in 1776, came from Surry. However, like so many other Surry natives, he became a city boy. After serving as Jefferson's secretary in Paris after the Revolution, he never went back to farming. As they sang in World War I, "How Ya Gonna Keep 'Em Down on the Farm, After They've Seen Paree?"

As part of Southside's black belt, made up of a dozen counties where blacks outnumber whites, Surry in my youth was one of Virginia's poorest. But recently it has impressed the world with its progress. The building of Virginia Power's nuclear power plant on Hog Island and the involvement of blacks in the county's government have helped Surry lift itself by its own bootstraps.

Today, Surry is one of a few American counties with a predominantly black government: black supervisors, county manager, county attorney, and others. Thanks to their moderation and the goodwill of Surry's whites, they have improved education, social services, and job opportunities. The county is an example of the amicable rice relations that John Marshall noted in the

140

Smithfield Times

James River ferry was started in 1925 by Captain A.F. Jester. To celebrate its 50th anniversary in 1975, antique automobiles crossed on the ferry, now operated by the state.

Virginia of the 1820s. It's making progress.

A Surry landowner once turned down an oil-driller's option to explore for oil on his land. "Why?" asked the oilman. "'Cause you might find it," the Surryman replied.

Much of that rural contentment obviously survives, among both whites and blacks. County residents still prefer their Jamestown-Scotland ferry to a bridge, which they fear would urbanize their county ("Like Gloucester," they shrug) and open its highways to get-rich-quick developers. Most Surry folk I know even say they enjoy that 20-minute ferry ride, though service is frequently disrupted by fog, river ice, or equipment failure. "The ferry gives me time to read the paper and catch my breath!" one Surry commuter to Williamsburg tells me.

Today the Jamestown ferry is the only such service left in Virginia of the many that operated before bridges and tunnels became popular. It's a money-losing operation for Virginia, recouping only about $500,000 of the $3,000,000 that it costs the state each year. But to old-fashioned Virginians, it seems to fit the rural environment of Jamestown, which it passes dozens of times daily on its 20-minute voyage between Glass House Point and Surry County.

In any case, I'll continue to enjoy romantic forays into Surry, Isle of Wight, Smithfield, and the rest of "the old country," as transplanted ex-Southsiders call it. That farm country may not offer the urban pleasures of the Peninsula—stores, theaters, ABC stores, French restaurants—but it has compensations of its own. Stoplights are few, and most folks are polite. They cure the best hams and bacon in the country, and they still make homemade rolls and biscuits.

Most of all, I like the self-reliance of people who, like Thoreau, march to the beat of their own drum. In a world that is losing its local differences, it's good to have individualists who hold out against conformity. The spirit of John Randolph of Roanoke is still alive south of the James.

Ferry from Jamestown to Surry County across the James is last to survive in Tidewater.

45. *The Great Storm of 1933*

THE VIRGINIA COAST has been mercifully free of most natural calamities except for the hurricanes which blow in every now and then in summer or fall. Among the worst have been Hurricane Hazel in October 1954, Camille in August 1969, and David in September 1979.

The fiercest I remember was Agnes in 1933.

Of course, the worst of all didn't hit Virginia. It was the Galveston hurricane of 1900, which caused 6,000 deaths. It was the severest natural disaster ever to befall the United States. In recent years hurricanes have been few on the Virginia coast.

Though the "official" hurricane season in the Atlantic is June 1 through November 30, the worst usually come in September and October. They result chiefly from ocean storms from the south Atlantic and Caribbean, but they're more destructive if they happen to hit the coast at high tide.

We've had fewer and milder hurricanes in recent years because a change in sun spots has altered world weather patterns. Certainly the worst was the one that hit Tidewater back in August 1933 called Agnes. Its high water did great damage, even knocking out Newport News' power plant. I was working on *The Times-Herald* that summer before going off to college, and we heroically produced a tiny, four-page handset *Times-Herald* on a hand press. It's a keepsake.

Hurricanes are felt around the world, but they're called "typhoons" in the Pacific, "cyclones" in the Indian Ocean, and "willy-willys" in Australia. The word "hurricane" comes from the West Indian "huracan," meaning evil spirit or great wind.

Up at VPI they've compiled records of Virginia's weather going back to John Smith's day. Early settlers recorded hurricanes, floods, droughts, and even earthquakes. One of the worst James River floods occurred in the 1770s, submerging the village of Varina on the Henrico County shore and washing away the isthmus that had linked Jamestown to the mainland.

As you'd expect, deaths from hurricanes have declined in recent years because of advance weather forecasts and warnings. The Office of Emergency Management keeps track of oncoming hurricanes and alerts the affected area.

Today's hurricanes create much worse damage than formerly because of the many resorts and cottages built in recent decades along the Atlantic and its estuaries. In Florida, I was told that insurers now require that the floor of the insured shore properties be 13 feet above mean low tide.

Recurring hurricanes have altered Virginia's geography these past recorded 380 years. Many Virginia towns that started with waterfront docks and warehouses were repeatedly damaged by hurricanes. Such was the case, for example, in the now extinct Gloucester Town, which stood in colonial times at Gloucester Point, opposite Yorktown.

Geographers tell us that coastline is always being altered by winds, waves and currents. Usually shore dwellers lose ground, even without hurricanes. Watermen tell me many Peninsula areas erode an average of a foot a year unless bulkheads or riprap are erected.

But Americans are willing to pay and risk a lot to live on the water. Many new beach houses are being built on pilings well above the shoreline in order to be insurable. Expensive beach houses are rising in profusion at Virginia Beach, Ocean View and Sandbridge. At the Rudee Inlet area of Virginia Beach I saw many, some built in Victorian Revival style and some in what I'd call Beach Bauhaus. They reflect California and Florida architectural innovations. Some are mansions, not cottages.

The Mariners' Museum gives safety rules for hurricanes: "Leave low-lying areas," "If local authorities recommend evacuation, you should move," "Board, tape or shutter windows" and "Stay indoors during the hurricane."

Daily Press

Waterfront cottages were demolished in 1933 by waves at Buckroe Beach, which never recovered from it.

Glimpses of Tidewater Life 145

Daily Press

Trolley and autos were marooned by high water in August 1933 by hurricane waters on Queen Street in Hampton.

46. *Ocean Shipping Days*

A SAN FRANCISCO WRITER named Max Miller captured the romance of ships in 1932 with his bestseller, *I Cover the Waterfront*. A popular song of that title was the rage when I was a college freshman in 1934–35. I view our Virginia waterways as our greatest civic asset, and full of romance to boot.

I got to know the Newport News waterfront as a C&O pier worker in the summers from 1932 to 1934 and later as a ships' news reporter for *The Times-Herald* while I was in college. The C&O and its piers hummed with activity.

In those days, the Old Dominion and Merchants and Miners coastal lines sent many cargo ships to Newport News, while transatlantic lines came less frequently. The terminals shipped out tobacco, grain and coal. Incoming cargo included bauxite, coffee, rubber and bananas.

My C&O job was unloading incoming freight on the piers and loading it in freight cars destined for inland cities. It was a rush job every night, for the big freight train was scheduled to pull out of Newport News shortly after midnight on its way west. Delays were costly.

I bossed a gang of four laborers, who located shipments of freight in accordance with waybills handed to me each night. Then they trucked or carried the freight to the freight car destined for the indicated city. When my gang and the others finished up, the pier was clear of merchandise. Then the cars were sealed and the powerful engine took them in tow for the trip west.

River Road in Newport News then ran from Pier A to 10th Street and thence to the coal piers on Point Breeze. It had been a riotous area of saloons, and seamen's dives, but by the time I came along they had been replaced by ship chandlers' and ship's agents' offices. These included Funch, Edye and Company; the U.S. Shipping Company; the Holland-American Line; and Norton Lilly and Company. I especially remember such agents as T. Parker Host, E.D.J. Luning, and Allan Hoffman.

Working at night on the waterfront was exciting. I came to work at 5 P.M. on the streetcar, occasionally encountering drunken sailors returning to their ships. Sometimes police patrol wagons, called "black Marias," roared down River Road to arrest miscreants on 18th Street, then a rundown neighborhood. I walked home at midnight to save a 50 cent taxi fare.

We who worked the night shift enjoyed a strange camaraderie. About 9 P.M. we knocked

Newport News yard was busy at lunchtime in 1919, when horsedrawn vans sold quick lunches.

off for 20 minutes to eat our bag suppers. I generally ate mine under a giant outdoor light at the river end of Pier 6, where we worked.

In those years, when the United States and Great Britain dominated merchant shipping, many major lines served Newport News. "The average local citizen does not realize the extent of the foreign shipping," wrote Harold Sniffen of the Mariners' Museum in 1946. He listed as Newport News ship services Cunard-White Star, Holland-American, the French Line, Swedish-American, North German-Lloyd, Red Star and others. In those days, more than 70 lines served Hampton Roads.

Sadly for Newport News, however, merchant shipping began to decline before World War II. High union costs put American shippers out of business, and air transport began to replace ocean shipping for perishable goods. Since World War II the U.S. has laid up nearly all its merchant ships.

The worst blow to Virginia shippers was the merger in 1963 of the C&O with the Baltimore and Ohio railway, forming what has become CSX. Because the B&O owned extensive freight facilities in Baltimore, CSX continues to give preference to that port over Newport News.

Additionally, CSX has created more modern

containerized cargo facilities at Baltimore than it offers in Newport News. It also offers more advantageous shipping rates in Baltimore. The result is that Newport News has become chiefly a coal export terminal. We need freight and passengers.

Can Hampton Roads become a lively port again? Shippers think it can, if CSX and the Virginia Ports Authority push it.

I ponder these problems as I breathe the sea air at the bridge-tunnel entrance and admire from my car the great port of Hampton Roads. Will Newport News ever become "the harbor of a thousand ships" it was in my C&O workdays? I hope so.

Daily Press

Hampton Roads before World War II swarmed with ships like this Swedish freighter, loading at Newport News.

47. *How They Talk in Tidewater*

WHEN Dr. Bennett Green died at the University of Virginia in the early 1900s, he left money in his will for educating Virginia boys—preferably from "below Jeems's River," as the old man put it. He felt that the character of Virginia survived more strongly (at least in 1899, when he wrote) in the rural Southside counties than anywhere else in the Old Dominion. He thought Southside had kept the faith. That's still true, for industry, military bases, and tourism have changed the face of Virginia since Green's lifetime.

Only in the "Black Belt," which runs from Chesterfield County across the James from Richmond and then south to North Carolina, do I find people still keeping the old ways as farmers, fishermen, sawmill hands or meat processors. That area is old-fashioned and unchanged, compared with this high tech peninsula.

Of all Virginians, farmers below the James best perpetuate the lifestyle of plantation days. Slavery is dead, but share-cropping and farm tenantry are not. A kindly concern for one's neighbors survives in unchanged Southside counties, where whites and blacks work together in peanut and tobacco fields against drought and disappearing markets. Farming is an uphill battle.

What especially marks rural Virginia is its English. In Southside you encounter a Southern drawl that gets deeper the farther south you go. It's a soft speech which prolongs vowels ("Come he-yuh to Day-uddy.") and slights hard consonants like "g" and "r." "Good gracious" comes out "Goo-ud gra-uh-shuss."

That sort of speech fascinated Dr. Bennett Green, a scholarly physician from Warwick County, who published a book in 1899 called *A Word-Book of Virginia Folk-Speech*. It's long out of print but often used by professors of language.

Bennett Green was born on Mulberry Island, now part of Fort Eustis, in the mid-1800s and served as a Confederate Navy surgeon in the Civil War. He believed that untutored Tidewater Virginians of his era spoke truly Elizabethan English, perpetuated word-of-mouth by descendants of Jamestown settlers. After all, most of the Englishmen who first came to Virginia had been farmers in England's West Country. Dr. Green even went to England and talked to West Countrymen to compare their speech.

Green's findings, set forth in his book, that many words, locutions, and idioms from Shakespeare's day survive in the speech of Virginians, especially the untutored. When we say "I'm right tired" or "I reckon I'll go," we're speaking archaic English. We also use words like "Mind you" for "Take note" and "I'll be there directly," which means "when I get around to it."

Old-timers in Smithfield are apt to say "The weather is fairing off" or "I don't fault you for that." People there "feel poorly" and describe wimps as "Just breath and britches." The depth of ill-temper is to be "as mean as old Jeffrys," which goes back to the 17th century cruelties of Lord George Jeffrys, a hanging judge of the Bloody Assizes.

The speech habits of southside Virginia are heavily colored by the dialect of the many rural blacks who live there. In fact, what's called the Southern accent begins to show up below the James and to intensify southward through the Carolinas into the deep South.

Inelegance wasn't necessarily ignorance in bygone Virginia. Douglas Freeman used "ain't" in familiar conversation, though he knew better. In the Virginia of Freeman's youth, old-fashioned people still used it and cited Shakespeare to justify it.

All over America, regional speech is colored by ethnic roots; African, German, Italian, Polish, or what-have-you. Much of ours in Virginia came over with the blacks, who began arriving in Virginia in 1619. More regionalisms entered the

Cotton is growing again in Tidewater counties south of the James, where summers are long.

Author's collection

Outdoor baptisms were popular among blacks early this century. This was in Amelia County.

Valley of Virginia in the 1720s with the influx of Germans and Scotch-Irishmen.

Ah, the Scotch-Irish! Their harsh, uncouth Scottish speech was at first far different from Tidewater's, but in 350 years they've been homogenized. However, we can forgive them all speech offenses for their Gaelic music and poetry. To them we owe the Appalachian ballads and folk songs which evolved into America's popular country music, bluegrass, and hillbilly you can hear at festivals in places like Galax and Abingdon as well as Nashville and Las Vegas.

Nashville's Grand Ole Opry owes much to those Celtic minstrels by way of Appalachia. It also owes something to African rhythms and to more recent Moog synthesizers and electronic banjoes and guitars.

Should we Southerners keep our accents, or should we talk like Walter Cronkite? I'm all for staying the way we are. The rest of the world may put down Southern talk, but lots of people copy us.

I remember a Richmond girl who was the belle of the college prom circuit in her Sweet Briar years. "Teh-yull me whu-ud I wanna heah," she'd coo over the phone from her Sweet Briar dormitory to her adoring swains. Now she lives in Connecticut where she has half the state talking Southern.

Governor John Dalton as a boy witnessed ship striking German mine off Virginia Beach in 1942.

Daily Press

48. *U-boats Scare Virginia Beach*

THE NAVAL WAR off Virginia in the 1940s was classified information long after World War II ended. Now it can be told. Monday, June 15, 1942, was a bright day at Virginia Beach. Bathers along the beach watched a convoy of U.S. merchant ships approaching Cape Henry, about to enter. All of a sudden an explosion offshore rocked the beach. A ship had been hit and was sinking!

Then a second ship exploded, giving off another cloud of smoke. Everybody on the beach focused on the convoy. Had German submarines dared to approach the capes and torpedoed ships on Norfolk's doorstep?

One spectator at the beach that day was 11-year-old John Dalton, later to be governor of Virginia.

"My parents and I were spending a week of vacation at the Albemarle Hall Hotel at 24th and Ocean Front when the convoy hit the mine field on June 15, 1942," Dalton wrote Edward Offley, the newspaperman who dug up the U-701 story. "We saw the ships go down and I remember one disabled ship which stayed out in the channel for some time before being taken on in to Norfolk."

The beach was littered with debris. Life rafts washed up on the beach, and the body of one dead sailor was brought to the Coast Guard Station immediately adjacent to the Albemarle Hall . . ."

The sinkings were thought to be the work of a German sub, and the Navy sent out ships and planes to comb the waters and drop depth charges. However, no submarine could be found. A few days later, on June 21, the Navy concluded that floating enemy mines had struck the ships—not torpedoes. Reported a Navy spokesman in Washington, "Undoubtedly these mines were laid by an enemy submarine under the cover of darkness, when detection is extremely difficult."

They were right. The guilty submarine had been the U-boat 701. It had sneaked up to the Virginia Capes the night of June 13 and planted a series of mines along the channel into Hampton Roads. Two days later the convoy smashed into them.

Meanwhile, the U-701 had moved from Virginia Beach out into the Atlantic off the North Carolina coast. It was far away when its mines exploded. Under the command of Captain Horst Degen, it was sailing along on the surface near North Carolina's Outer Banks on July 7 when it was suddenly spotted by an Air Corps plane commanded by Lieutenant Harry Kane, of Kin-

152

ston, a small town in North Carolina.

The German skipper had thought he was safe on the surface because of low clouds overhead which made U-boat detection difficult. However, Kane and his plane crew were flying low. They spotted the U-701 through a fortunate break in the clouds. That was it for the Germans.

After the German skipper and six other survivors of the 40-man crew had been picked up in the Atlantic 49 hours after the sinking, they were brought to the Naval Air Station at Norfolk for questioning. From them the Navy learned that the U-701 had planted the mines. Wrote John Dalton years later, after reading the newspaper account, "Even thought I was not quite 11 years old at the time of this incident. I remember the ships sinking off Virginia Beach when they struck the mines almost as if it were yesterday."

"We had blackout curtains on the windows at the hotel, but Captain Degen was watching us anyway on June 13. If you correspond again with Captain Degen and Lieutenant Kane, you might let them know that a future governor of Virginia was a spectator to a part of their rendezvous with destiny," Dalton wrote Edward Offley.

Virginia Beach's German mine warfare has recently been studied by Alpheus J. Chewning, a captain in the Virginia Beach fire department. In 1994 he wrote *The Approaching Storm: U Boats Off the Virginia Coast During World War II,* describing the U-701 incident and others. Chewning corresponded with Degen, who was saved from the Atlantic after his submarine sank and brought to Norfolk as a prisoner of war. In Norfolk, Degen met and complimented the American pilot who had sunk his submarine.

Another long-kept secret of World War II is the existence of the anti-submarine net which blocked Hampton Roads' main channel at Old Point against marauding Nazi and Japanese U-boats. The Navy refuses to confirm its existence, but some say an enemy sub was caught in it.

Confirmation that the net did exist comes from no less than British actor Alec Guinness, now Sir Alec, whose biography was published as *Blessings in Disguise.* Guinness was a British naval officer during World War II, and his small warship got caught in the net one night in 1941, before the United States entered the war. Nobody was hurt, but Guinness was profoundly embarrassed.

At that time Uncle Sam was giving warships to the British under President Franklin Roosevelt's lend-lease program, and Guinness and his British crew had come to the United States to pick up an LCI (landing craft, infantry) and sail it to the war zone. The young actor, nervous in

Author's collection

German U-boat U-701 laid mines at Virginia Beach but was later destroyed off North Carolina.

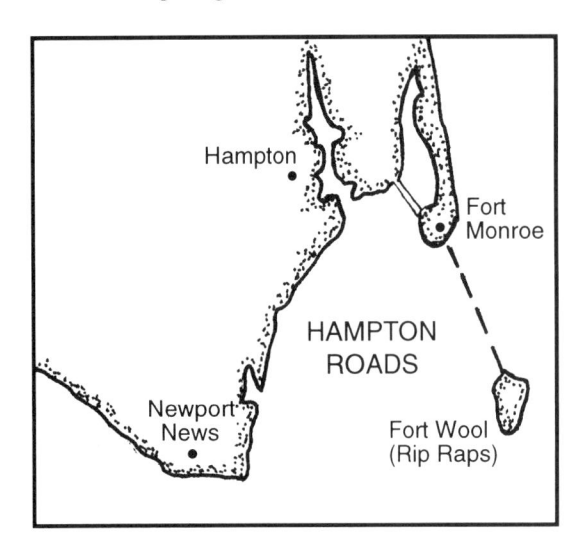

Secret antisub net was strung in World War II from Fort Monroe across water to Fort Wool.

his first command, was to take the LCI to North Africa for the British campaign against Field Marshal Erwin Rommel's Afrika Corps. It was a rushed trip.

"We sailed from New York and straight into trouble," Guinness writes. "In Chesapeake Bay, across the entrance to the estuary of the James river, there was a great defense boom. Night had fallen, weather conditions were appalling, there were no navigational aids (I could spread out the excuses), and I managed to get one third of my ship straddled across the boom designed, or so they thought, to stop penetration by the enemy."

According to wartime rumors on the Peninsula, the boom—a floating line of buoys which supported the metal net—stretched between Fort Monroe and the Rip Raps (Fort Wool) and from there across to the Norfolk side. The Rip Raps, a small island in Hampton Roads built by the Army as Fort Calhoun in the 1820s, is now attached to the Hampton Roads Bridge-Tunnel.

Nobody apparently told Lieutenant Guinness about the submarine net. After all, it was a war secret.

"We struggled off our spider's web in an hour or so," Guinness reports, "thanks to the patience of the engine-room staff. . . . Visibility was nil, so having backed away from the boom, I dropped anchor. The first light of day was an alarming revelation: Together with half a dozen of LCIs, we had anchored in the middle of a mine field. The tide had gone down, and the mines could be seen a foot below the surface, swaying like sinister black balloons."

That World War II floating boom to deter the enemy in Hampton Roads revived a plan that was proposed by the builder of Fort Monroe in the 1820s. He was French General Simon Bernard, who was retained by the United States during James Monroe's presidency to design a dozen forts along the Atlantic Coast to avert a repetition of Britain's naval attacks in the War of 1812. In that war, the British invaded Hampton in 1813 and tried unsuccessfully to burn Norfolk.

The deepest of the two main Hampton Roads channels is Hampton Channel, which comes close to the shoreline at Old Point. For that reason, General Bernard conceived the building of a smaller fort on the far side of the channel so a "log-boom" could be stretched across in wartime. There were no submarines then, so only surface ships had to be dealt with.

Unfortunately, the sandy shoal the Army chose to name Fort Calhoun continued to sink, and its completion was long delayed. When young Lieutenant Robert E. Lee was assigned by the Army engineers to Fort Monroe in the 1830s, his assignment was to finish the fort.

President Monroe and War Secretary John C. Calhoun came down from Washington to inspect progress on the forts. No doubt they were concerned by cost overruns at Fort Calhoun. The isolated site drew visits from many impressed VIPs, including President John Tyler, who stayed there in seclusion after the death of his first wife, Letitia.

Fort Calhoun was renamed Fort Wool during the Civil War and was used as an observation station to detect Confederate movements in Norfolk before that city was taken by Federal forces.

After World War II Fort Wool was deeded to Virginia, which promptly gave it to Hampton. It is now exhibited to tourists on sightseeing cruises, which pass over the spot where Lieutenant Alec Guinness once spent a very unpleasant night.

49. *Sending Our Boys to Fight Hitler*

SCATTERED through the woods near Williamsburg-Newport News International Airport are the fragmented remains of streets laid in World War II for the Army's Camp Patrick Henry. That's where hundreds of thousands of GIs in 1944 and 1945 encamped a day or so under heavy security waiting to board troop transports in Hampton Roads to fight Hitler in Europe.

Now the camp is replaced by bustling new offices and subdivisions, but one person who well remembers it is Mrs. Clyde Roller, a Texas concert pianist who returned to the Peninsula recently. "What a thrill it was to visit Hampton and Newport News again," she said.

How did a Texas pianist find herself in Patrick Henry in wartime? Young Mrs. Roller (then Miss Moreland Kortkamp) had signed up as part of a string trio and two vocalists for a USO troop tour. She was just out of Juilliard Conservatory in New York and had taken a half-dozen medical shots and been issued a green drab USO uniform.

The USO troupe reached Patrick Henry after an overnight train trip from New York. With Miss Kortkamp were 20 other USO women plus a few USO men. "Each day at Patrick Henry was filled with drills, lectures on Army protocol, and equipment issuance," she told me. Then the group entrained to the Newport News cargo piers to board the Army transport *Billy Mitchell* in strict secrecy. After nine days on shipboard during a zig-zag crossing of the South Atlantic, they reached Casablanca.

The pianist's USO troupe for months was to entertain American soldiers in the North African campaign. After Sicily and Anzio were invaded, the Army and the troupe moved to the Italian peninsula. "We gave concerts in opera houses, wine cellars, airports, theaters, and Army camps," she recalled. For awhile they camped near Florence with General Mark Clark's Fifth Army.

Returning to the United States for rest and recreation in September, 1944, Miss Kortkamp met two Virginia musicians who became her friends. They were pianist Marjorie Mitchell of Charlottesville and violinist Elizabeth Chapman of Hampton. They remained close as long as they lived.

When the USO hired Moreland Kortkamp for a second tour in 1944, it sent her back to Europe to accompany a troupe of Ballet Russe dancers from New York. "I was emcee, manager of the troupe, and played piano solos between ballets,"

Soldiers returning to Camp Patrick Henry in World War II line up for long-distance calls.

Miss Kortkamp remembers.

"Again we were sent to Patrick Henry," Mrs. Roller recalled. "Again we went through a week of secret training. But this time we crossed the Atlantic from Newport New to Naples, once again following the Fifth Army." Soon the Fifth was joined by the 12th Air Force, which had been brought from England to Italy to help invade France after D-Day.

After Allied troops landed in Normandy and, with Russian aid, backed Hitler to the wall, the Allies began to plan for V-E Day, to accept the surrender of Germany and Italy. "We were in Sicily in the Spring of 1945," Mrs. Roller recalls, "and on May 8, 1945, were flown back to Caserta, Italy, headquarters of the Mediterranean theater of operations, to join other groups for a big show to celebrate V-E Day."

After Germany surrendered on May 7, 1945, Miss Kortkamp's USO group was flown to Paris to perform. Then they did so in Belgium, Holland, and Germany.

"We returned just before Japan surrendered on V-J Day, September 2, 1945. This time we celebrated the surrender in Times Square in New York City."

Today little evidence of those tremendous wartime troop movements remains in Newport News. It seems destined to be remade during every war.

50. *Discovering Alexandria*

THERE ARE TWO Alexandrias. One was founded by Alexander the Great in 332 B.C. on Egypt's Nile delta. The other was created by Scottish settlers in Virginia in A.D. 1749 on the lands of John Alexander near present-day Washington, D.C. Alexandria Number Two recently has come into its own as one of America's most charming and historic colonial survivals.

"These Virginians give themselves airs," complained one early British governor, and Alexandrians were prime offenders. Profits from the town's trans-atlantic wheat and tobacco trade went into elaborate brick and frame structures of Old Town, as the colonial area is called today. Even warehouses (now converted into boutiques and import shops) were made of handmade brick.

Agricultural and shipping profits continued to expand the town until post-Civil War times. It became a big port. Alexandria's subtlest charm is its mixture of old and new, treasured and trashy, characteristic of most old cities. Bookstores, antique shops and restaurants crop up between high-rise banks and office buildings, and mom-and-pop grocery stores survive next door to fine mansions.

In addition to its other assets, Alexandria can boast of being George Washington's hometown. Only six miles from Mount Vernon, it was the hub of Washington's business life from the time he became a planter in 1747 until his death in 1799. Here he built a townhouse for overnight stops, and here he and Martha worshipped in Christ Church, danced at Gadsby's Tavern and dined with friends and relatives in Georgian mansions that still line Oronoco, St. Asaph and other colonial streets.

In George Washington's time, Alexandria's city fathers drank and dined at John Gadsby's brick Tavern and City Hotel, which had grown from the modest Mason's Ordinary. In addition to Washington, other famous people enjoyed its hospitality. When hard times came in 1879, Gadsby's closed its doors for ninety-seven years. Dwarfed by Washington, D.C. and shorn of shipping, the old city grew but little for the next half century.

In the 1930s, residents and outsiders began to buy and restore Alexandria's old houses. The movement was led by Mrs. Gay Montague Moore, the farsighted daughter of a Virginia governor, who is acclaimed today as Old Town's godmother. In 1976 the city reopened Gadsby's

Alexandria's tone is set by its well-attended Christ Church, which Washington once attended.

Tavern as part of its Bicentennial program, and it has been maintained since as a restaurant and museum.

The growth of the nation's capital has also contributed to Alexandria's expansion since World War II. Commuters flocked in, and builders were hard-pressed to create expressways to keep pace. The stream of former U.S. Route 1 traffic now circumvents Old Town on Interstate 95, and a Metro subway station further expedites transportation with an Alexandria stop adjoining the Masonic Memorial, west of Old Town's core.

Although Alexandria started life as a seaport, its waterfront has been quieted by the rise of commuters and the decline of Potomac shipping. Old docks, rundown and unused, have been torn down, and a new sort of dockside has begun to emerge. Warehouses have blossomed into shops and restaurants, and luxury hotels and condominiums sprout steadily. Extensive waterfront improvement continues.

The Old Town that greets today's visitor hums with modern hotels and restaurants and even discos. Although shopping malls and apartments surround the old city, the romantic past persists in the inner enclave of columned porticos, graceful stairways and black-green shutters against russet brick. It also survives in costumed militia parades, bagpipe concerts and historical events galore.

On the city's main thoroughfare, Washington Street (once overrun by automobiles when it was part of U.S. Route 1 from D.C. westward), stand many of the city's major buildings. Among them: Christ Church, the Lyceum-Bicentennial Center and the 1793 Lloyd House, now the repository of the city's historic papers. Besides George Washington, early Alexandria had close associations with George Mason (who lived at nearby Gunston Hall and conceived the Virginia Bill of Rights) and with Richard Henry Lee (who proposed the Declaration of Independence in Philadelphia).

Another restored mansion, the Carlyle House, hosted the colonial governors of Massachusetts, New York, Pennsylvania, Maryland and Virginia when they met in 1755 to adopt a continental British strategy in the French and Indian Wars. Out of that meeting the British imposed the hated Stamp Act in 1765, bringing from Patrick Henry the first protests of the oncoming Revolution. The house is now open to sightseers.

Much of Alexandria's nineteenth-century history centers around Robert E. Lee, who spent his youthful years in the city. Two former homes of Lee's father, Lighthorse Harry Lee (one on Cameron Street and the other on North Washington Street known as the Fendall-Lee House), are targets for the historically minded. Nearby, on

Oronoco Street, stands the Fitzhugh-Lee House, where Lee lived from age four to eighteen, when he entered West Point. Lafayette and Washington were both guests in the house in earlier years. Both the Fendall-Lee and Fitzhugh-Lee houses are open for visitors, as are several other Alexandria mansion of the period.

But the city was not home to mansions only. On tree-lined, cobblestoned Prince Street stand the modest and brightly painted apartments of Captain's Row, where skippers of ships that linked Alexandria with London, Liverpool, Glasgow and the Bahamas made their homes. On South Alfred Street, the Friendship Fire Engine Company (founded in 1774 with Washington as a member) is maintained by enthusiasts who delight in showing off its early hand-pumped fire engine and hose reel.

On South Fairfax, the bow-windowed Stabler-Leadbetter Apothecary Shop (opened in 1792 and operated as a drugstore until 1933) retains its archaic scales and rows of apothecary jars as exhibits. Here, where Washingtons and Lees once shopped for pills and potions, antiques of varying quality are sold.

Alexandria does not live altogether in the past. Gerald Ford called it home until he succeeded Richard Nixon as president and moved to the White House in 1974. Nixon lived there while a congressman, as have many other political figures and their families. The colonial Fendall-Lee House, now an exhibition building, was home for years to labor leader John L. Lewis. Cabinet member Dean Rusk and Admiral William F. "Bull" Halsey also chose Alexandria's tree-lined streets in preference to Washington.

Much of the city's charm lies in its waterfront, where schooners loaded grain for Caribbean ports and tobacco for Europe. Gradually deserted by commercial shippers after World War I, Alexandria's waterfront has become an oasis of

Prince Street's rowhouses typify the many brick lodgings on cobbled streets found in Alexandria.

pleasure-boat marinas, gourmet restaurants, craft shops, and hotels. In a burst of imagination a few years ago, the city converted the disused Navy Torpedo Factory—once the repository of seized Nazi war records—into an arts center with low-rent studios for artists and craftsmen.

Finding modern use for restored buildings is part of Alexandria's success. When the 1839 Lyceum faced destruction in 1975, the city persuaded the Virginia Bicentennial Commission to restore it as the Northern Virginia Bicentennial Center, now in use as a museum. Similarly, the frame house of William Ramsay, Alexandria's lord mayor in 1761, now houses the city's tour office.

Many of Alexandria's residents are young careerists who give a yuppie flavor to the old town. A few years ago, when Time-Life Books moved from New York into a fine new Alexandria building shaped like a Roman atrium, its youthful writers and editors attracted a new disco and lively bars.

A flock of new restaurants has descended on the city. Their ethnic diversity includes Southern cooking, Greek food, French cuisine, and Italian dining.

If the Father of his Country were to come back to Alexandria today, he would find much to startle him. Jetliners zoom over the Potomac every few moments, wall-to-wall autos crowd the streets, and subway trains rumble beneath streets where Revolutionists marched over 200 year ago. But he would also find himself very much at home in those beautiful old houses where the Revolutionary spirit was nurtured long ago. It is that age—the age of Washington and of our nation's birth—that Alexandria evokes.

Alexandria's harbor, once busy with wheat cargoes, now moors hundreds of pleasure boats.

Daily Press

The Red Fox Tavern at Middleburg claims to be the nation's oldest inn.

51. *Colonial Inns Are Still Going*

"NOTHING devised by the mind of man has given so much pleasure to mankind as an inn," wrote Samuel Johnson in eighteenth-century England, and he was right. More and more, travelers are discovering the delights of the fragrant and often historic public houses spread across the face of America, survivors of a leisurely and colorful past.

In Tidewater, Virginia, the ghosts of Jefferson, Madison, and other erstwhile taverners haunt a dozen or so eighteenth-century hostelries which flourish in that picturesque state. George Washington may have slept in many places, but he ate in even more.

From Williamsburg to Alexandria, where Gadsy's Tavern reopened in 1977 after a half-century's sleep, visitors are feasting on such colonial treats as game pie, scalloped oysters, syllabub, and English trifle. Three-tined forks, rattail spoons, and pistol-handled knives have reappeared at table, along with napkins tied at the chin. Eighteenth-century dining has been rediscovered, and cornbread, hot biscuits, ale in pewter mugs, and a lot of specialties that great-grandma enjoyed are again gracing tables.

Dining in Williamsburg at night, you can almost hear the barman call out, "Mind your p's and q's," as he did in those same cozy taverns in pre-Revolutionary days. Standing behind his half-shuttered wine and spirits bar—still in place today—he was warning diners to collect their pints and quarts of ale before he closed the bar. You can still get ale, but most modern diners settle for highballs and wine, even if they're less authentic eighteenth-century fare.

The best-known Tidewater taverns still serving meals are probably the King's Arms, Mrs. Campbell's, Chowning's, and Shields, all in Williamsburg. They've enjoyed the careful restoration which the Rockefellers lavished on every detail in that eighteenth-century capital. But many other old taverns still flourish in the Old Dominion.

At Smithfield, the Smithfield Inn, built in 1752, is a sort of vestal temple to the famous Smithfield ham. And in the hunt country of northern Virginia, the fame of Middleburg's Red Fox Tavern (1728) and Leesburg's Laurel Brigade (1759) are as familiar as Secretariat's pedigree.

Each of these inns has a story. Typical is Gadsby's Tavern on Alexandria's North Royal Street, which vies with the Old Club (built before

Chowning's was popular 18th century tavern reconstructed in Williamsburg.

1790) as the favorite colonial eatery of George Washington's hometown. Built about 1752 as the City Tavern, Gadsby's reached its zenith in Washington's lifetime. When John Gadsby took it over in 1796, the tavern had grown into the City Hotel and was known as "the best house of entertainment in America." Washington was entertained here at birthday balls, and he and Martha attended dancing assemblies in its ballroom. Five other presidents plus John Paul Jones, Aaron Burr, Francis Scott Key, and Henry Clay numbered among Gadsby's patrons.

Gadsby's offers an early American menu, served in paneled, eighteenth-century-style rooms. Its specialty is "General Washington's Favorite Duck," with fruit dressing and Madeira sauce.

A few miles away at Middleburg, the Red Fox Tavern spreads a bountiful table in a white colonial house that was originally called Chinn's Ordinary, built in 1728. During fox-hunting season the tavern and its Night Fox Pub are hangouts of the fox-hunting crowd, which includes locals and politicos from Washington. The Confederate hero Jeb Stuart stayed at the tavern during the Civil War, and President Kennedy held a press conference there.

In the dining room, a rustic atmosphere prevails; exposed beams, pine-paneled walls, painted stone fireplaces, and red-clothed tables.

At Leesburg awaits another colonial inn, the Laurel Brigade. Begun in 1766 as an ordinary—a public house serving all comers the hosts' "ordinary" fare—it was renamed after the Civil War for the northern Virginia brigade that fought under Confederate hero Turner Ashby. Its facade of weathered stone stands flush against Leesburg's main street, where country squires and city slickers gather on weekends to race horses and hunt foxes.

The Laurel Brigade has changed a lot since 1766—all for the better, apparently. In that year its rate was set by a county law: "Lodging on clean sheets, 6 shillings. Otherwise, nothing." Host Roy Flippo has preserved the informal ambience of a rural inn, relying on such familiar fare as country ham, Chesapeake bay flounder and crab. It is especially busy during the many hunt meets and point-to-point races which fill Warrenton's year.

Midway between Richmond and Petersburg on U. S. Route 1 lies Halfway House, whose English basement dining room has fed travelers since 1760, including Lafayette, Patrick Henry, and Ulysses S. Grant, who accepted the surrender of Lee's army at nearby Appomattox in 1865. One Halfway House patron was the terrible-tempered John Randolph of Roanoke, who dropped in while en route to and from sessions of Congress.

The Smithfield Inn grew up in America's ham-curing capital and takes advantage of the fact. The heavenly red ham tops the menu and can also be ordered with fried chicken. What's more, the inn's green vegetables are cooked with cured "side meat," in Southern fashion, and are served with stewed tomatoes, cornbread, and biscuits. Another entrée is Brunswick stew, which Virginians say originated in Brunswick County. The original recipe used squirrel, but the Smithfield version substitutes chicken.

The inn, built in 1752 to serve lawyers and litigants attending the Isle of Wight Courthouse (then next door to the inn), boasted a gaming house for patrons' pleasure.

Across the James in Williamsburg, the gustatory glories of the past are also making a brave stand. At the King's Arms Tavern on Duke of Gloucester Street, one sits amid candlelight while waiters in knee hose and breeches flourish Sally Lunn bread, oyster pye, and napkins the size of card-table covers. Then, protected against stain, the diner makes his way through four or five heavenly courses.

Each of the four Williamsburg taverns has its specialties. The King's Arms—most elaborate of the four—offers ham, roast beef, and lamb chops. Nearby Chowning's Tavern features Brunswick stew, Welsh rabbit, and steaks. At Christiana Campbell's Tavern, seafood is the thing. In 1989 Colonial Williamsburg opened Shields Tavern on Duke of Gloucester Street, serving eighteenth-century-style meals.

After a day of travel, what can be more pleasant than to sit with friends in a well-appointed tavern, sipping your drink and contemplating delights to come? The inns of Tidewater cultivate those pleasures to the hilt.

Washington feted Revolutionary officers at Williamsburg's Campbell's Tavern.

Colonial Williamsburg

52. *Those Heroic Watermen*

IF YOU'VE EVER CAUGHT an eel on a fishing line, you know what a mess that slimy, snakelike fish can make of your hook and fishing line.

But in Holland, the despised Chesapeake Bay scavenger is relished as a delicacy. In Dutch cities, smoked and pickled eels are sold from street stands and eaten by rich and poor.

I've long known that many Virginia eels are shipped abroad, so I asked the Virginia Institute of Marine Science at Gloucester Point about it. I learned that Europeans pay good money for our ugly eels. It turns out that eels are shipped abroad from Chesapeake live, frozen, or cooked. Most of Virginia's eels are exported by a wholesale seafood dealer of Westmoreland County. Others are bought by dealers and shipped from Maryland and North Carolina.

The Westmoreland firm ships 700 tons of eels to Holland a year. "Most eels caught by sport fishermen are thrown back," says Herbert Austin of VIMS's Gloucester laboratory.

Atlantic eels originate in the Sargasso Sea, that part of the ocean south of Bermuda and 1,000 miles east of Florida. Eel larvae begin traveling coastward immediately after hatching and reach the Chesapeake's coastal waters about one year old. They swim close to the bottom.

Millions of small eels, called elvers, enter Virginia tidal estuaries and marshes each spring. At this stage they are tiny, transparent, and big eaters. They mature in brackish waters. When large enough to spawn, mature eels swim back through the Capes to the Sargasso Sea, where they spawn and start another life cycle.

Eels in Virginia waters feed on small fish, fish eggs, small crustaceans, and carrion. They grow as long as three feet at maturity. Because of their mucous covering and their unusual intestinal structure, they're hard to clean. The chief American sales for eels are in ethnic markets in the North. Scandinavians call them "all," while Italians call them "anguilla," and the Greeks "cheli."

Most Chesapeake Bay eels are caught in eel traps or fine-mesh fish nets. At the eel exporting plant at Mount Holly in Westmoreland County they are bought live by thousands from watermen, packed in ice, and shipped to Holland the same day via Dulles or Baltimore International airports. Eel shippers in Maryland and North Carolina compete with Virginia, but the eels must be tested for chemicals that might make them unsafe by European culinary standards.

Another Virginia seafood in growing demand

Virginia Division of Tourism

Tangier Islander with dog makes run to check his floats and collect night's softcrabs.

abroad is the soft crab. It is a favored dish nowadays in Japan, Hong Kong, Singapore, and parts of Europe. William DuPaul of the Virginia Institute of Marine Science at Gloucester says thousands are bought by Maryland exporters each summer and shipped overseas frozen, "The soft crab is one of the few seafoods that freezes well," DuPaul told me.

Some soft crabs are now available in winter. They are rock crabs, different from the familiar blue crabs of Virginia, and are caught by winter dredgers as a by-catch while dredging in deep water for blue crabs near the Virginia Capes. Rock crabs shed and become soft in winter, unlike blue crabs, but they do so only for about six weeks.

165

waters. Virginia dogfish, or sand sharks, were also exported to Europe in the early 1980s. Few Americans eat sharks knowingly, though some shark is sold unidentified as fish sticks.

Marine scientists think Tidewater has a good future as a producer of seafoods, some of them once commercially unexploited. I can see a growing future for Hampton Roads as an exporter of eels, soft crabs, dogfish, squid, and other catches, along with already popular Chesapeake oysters, crab, and finfish.

Like Captain John Smith in 1608, I'm impressed with the variety of the Chesapeake's fish. Smith listed them as sturgeon and "clampes" as well as "brettes, mullets, white Salmonds, Trowts, Soles, Plaice, Herrings, Rockfish, Eeles, Shades, Crabs, Shrimps, Oysters, Cocles, and Muscles."

Now, in the age of airplanes and freezers, we're shipping them everywhere.

Deep sea fishing in the Atlantic is popular from Eastern Shore and Virginia Beach.

Virginia Division of Tourism

Virginia Division of Tourism

Favorite haunt of watermen is Poquoson on York, which has well-known seafood restaurants.

Tidewater watermen are also exporting squid, DuPaul says, one species called "summer squid" and another "winter squid." Both differ from the Monterey squid of the California coast. Europeans call them "calmari" or "kalamari" and eat them fried and in stew.The Virginia Marine Products Board in Newport News is trying to expand the market for these and other Virginia saltwater products. To illustrate the benefits of marketing, it points to the popularity of monkfish, once the despised angler fish, and of sea squab, the meat of the blow toad, once common in Virginia

53. *Commuters Transform Tidewater*

IF YOU LIVE on the Eastern Shore, you're bound to cross Chesapeake Bay to mainland cities like Hampton, Newport News and Norfolk. In the days before the Chesapeake Bay Bridge-Tunnel, that usually meant a glamorous voyage aboard a big white steamer out of Baltimore or Washington, which docked at Cape Charles to take passengers to Old Point or Norfolk.

A voyager in those river boat days was Spencer Wise, who grew up in Craddockville in Accomack County and later taught at Christopher Newport University in Newport News. He writes of "Daytripping by Steamer" in *Chesapeake Bay Magazine.* Boy, were those the good old days!

But travel then, before Virginia had good highways and bridges, was painfully slow. The Wise family had to get up before dawn to reach Old Point or Norfolk by midday when the SS *Pennsylvania* and the SS *Maryland* carried passengers and freight for the old NYP&N ("Nippinen")—the New York, Philadelphia and Norfolk Railroad Company. The bay boat service ended February 28, 1953, when the SS *Elisha Lee* made the last run between Cape Charles-Old Point-Norfolk.

Now the onetime Government Dock where bay steamers landed alongside the Chamberlin at Old Point has been torn down. We're in an air-and-auto age.

The Wise family started its journey to Old Point by boarding the NYP&N train at Exmore for a 23-mile ride to Cape Charles. About 7 A.M. they went aboard the bayside steamer after it arrived from Baltimore—either the SS *Pennsylvania* or SS *Maryland* or their occasional relief boat, the older *New York.* These storied ships and others linked Eastern Shore farmers and fishermen efficiently for 69 years with the cities of Virginia and the north.

On the pier side, gangs of men were working furiously to load the mail, baggage and express form the train onto the boat," Wise recalls of the scene at Cape Charles. "Only 20 minutes were scheduled for transferring the contents of five or six (rail) cars." Soon the gangplank was hauled in and the ship headed down Cherrystone Creek, crossed Plantation Flats through a dredged channel, and headed for Thimble Shoal Light across Chesapeake Bay near Hampton.

"Breakfast in the ship's dining saloon was one of the trip's treats. Breakfast was less than $1, leaving money for a tip. Fingerbowls were

Ferries linked Newport News with Norfolk Naval Base from 1907 till tunnel opened in 1957.

brought by the waiter along with the check, puzzling children who'd never see them.

"By the time breakfast was over, the Hampton shoreline and even some of the larger buildings there were visible," Wise writes.

> We were approaching "the Horseshoe," dreaded by many passengers and especially by my female relatives. The Horseshoe is a large shoal extending eastward into the Bay from the Hampton shore. If any swells were coming into the Bay . . . the boats could roll appreciably as they crossed the . . . shallow water.

The wharf at Old Point was one of the busiest on the Atlantic, serving both regional Bay steamers and smaller river steamers which tied the James and York rivers and Mobjack Bay. Some passengers arriving at Old Point boarded the trolley for Peninsula stops while others journeyed by taxi across Mill Creek to Phoebus and there boarded the C&O, which provided passenger service to Newport News and westward to the Great Lakes. Some stayed at the Chamberlin Hotel or its antecedent, the Hygeia, to take the waters at Old Point.

"In the center of Government Wharf stood a building that housed the waiting rooms, the ticket office, and mail and express storage space," Wise writes. At Old Point ships often loaded oysters form J.S. Darling or crabmeat from the McMenamin plant, both in Hampton. I recall once seeing several huge sea turtles, alive and kicking helplessly on their backs, awaiting shipment north to be made into stew.

When the Wise family continued by boat to Norfolk, young Spencer noted the big warships at Norfolk's naval base and the noisy coal-dumping piers of the C&O at Newport News and the Virginian Railway at Norfolk. The return from Norfolk to Cape Charles in late afternoon was equally pleasant. "Soon after we left Old Point we went down to dinner," Wise writes. "I can still remember the dining room with the later afternoon sun astern and Old Point receding into the distance. As always, the service was flawless."

Occasionally in the 1920s the Wise family drove its Model T from their home at Craddocksville to the Cape Charles dock, helped railway employees drain gas from the tank as a safety measure, and then watched the car being loaded on board. At Old Point, the tank was refilled, and the family was then off to tour the Peninsula.

Wise recalls that in 1928 the SS *Virginia Lee,* a new bay steamer, came on to supplement the *Maryland* and the *Pennsylvania.* In 1944 came the SS *Elisha Lee,* which replaced the older *Delmarva.* Several Bay steamers were requisitioned by Uncle Sam in World War II to carry troops in the United States and abroad. Bay shipping was never the same after that war.

Spencer Wise went on to college at Virginia Tech and got a degree in agriculture. After serving in the Navy and trying his hand at farming, he moved to the Peninsula and taught. Like most Virginians of his generation, his life was enhanced by growing up in the country and traveling frequently over the beautiful bays and rivers of the Chesapeake region.

Daily Press

Old Bay liner City of Richmond *docks at Old Point en route from Baltimore to Norfolk.*

Beavers are numerous around the Chickahominy, where they cut trees to dam waters.

Virginia Gazette

54. *Where Sea Meets Shore*

Virginia Gazette

LIFE ON VIRGINIA' SHORES offers a year-round saga of nature's moods. Visible are eagles, blackbirds, and many species of water and shore birds. No less common are wild deer, whose number has greatly increased in recent years, to the alarm of farmers and gardeners. Exotic egrets, herons, and loons appear, too.

Underwater the life cycle of countless seafoods retells the story of the strong preying on the weak. Crabs eat plankton, toadfish and eels eat soft crabs, and larger fish prey on toadfish and eels.

Belatedly, mankind realizes the need for preserving the wetlands.

Young deer look for spring greens in a pine forest not far from Jamestown.

Glimpses of Tidewater Life 171

Daily Press photo by Thom Slater

Willis Clark of Newport News uses fishtail bait in hopes of catching a hard crab.

Turkey buzzards congregate on a winter's day, close to the York River.

An Indian River egret looks for prey along the marsh shore.

Virginia Gazette photo by Maria Anderson

Daily Press photo by Michael D. Asher

55. *Saving the Marshes*

BILL SNYDER lives near Jamestown and keeps his eyes on the world around him. A native of Newport News, he worked 40 years in the shipyard before moving to a woodland retreat in James City County. Like Thoreau, whose greatest pleasure was living on Walden Pond and watching the seasons, Snyder's passion is nature. He's wandered all over James City and York, noting the migrations of birds and the haunts of eagles, beavers, deer and other creatures.

"We Peninsulans are surrounded by a wealth of birds and animals that we must protect," Snyder says.

He's written three books about birds, animals and plants of the Peninsula, and he conducts guided tours for amateur naturalists and historians. At 80, he's vigorous and active.

Many species of animal life are increasing, Snyder tells me, including wild turkeys, deer, raccoons and squirrels. He credits that fact to our increasing awareness of nature and Virginia's Non-Game Wildlife and Endangered Species Program. He's not opposed to hunting but prefers animal-watching. He keeps notes of his observations and gives these to wildlife agencies. I met Bill Snyder when I ran Jamestown Festival Park from 1957 to 1980. He lives nearby on Powhatan Creek. He's read the accounts by John Smith, George Percy and other Jamestown settlers, and

Author's collection

From his wilderness home on Jamestown's Powhatan Creek, Bill Snyder watches animals.

he marvels at the persistence of the wildlife the first settlers noted on their arrival from England.

If you like birds and animals, Snyder recommends any of a dozen preserves where you can see them: Jamestown, Newport News City Park, York River State Park, Williamsburg's Waller Mill Park, Hog Island in the James, Chickahominy Wildlife Area in Charles City and Ragged Island Wildlife Area near the Isle of Wight end of James River Bridge.

Of all nearby game preserves, Hog Island is probably the most exciting. An estimated 10,000 wild geese and countless ducks winter there, flying south from Canada in fall and returning in summer. Rarities like goshawks and barnacle geese are spotted there. Many raise young along Hog Island's streams and the James.

Another interesting wildlife area is Jamestown. Swampy and picturesque, its marshes along the Thoroughfare and nearby Powhatan Creek are full of muskrats and shore birds. On an outing there, I saw several varieties of osprey plus mallards that have been fed by shore dwellers and domesticated.

The protected 1,550 acres of Jamestown contain about 1,000 deer. Some venture close to the Visitor Center at dusk. There are also night-prowling raccoons, possums, muskrats, woodchucks and rabbits. A five-mile Wilderness Road around the island brings you close to nesting wildfowl. Red-headed woodpeckers, ospreys and an occasional eagle nest on the island.

In John Smith's history of Virginia, he listed himself as seeing "conies" (rabbits), deer, turkeys, bears, foxes, squirrels, otters, waterfowl and wild pigeons. He described Powhatan as "hung with manie chaynes of great pearles about his neck and covered with a great covering of raccoon skins and all the tayles hanging by."

Virginia's first settlers also found buffalo and

Virginia Division of Tourism

Wild horses breed in marshes and are rounded up yearly at Chincoteague Pony Penning.

Virginia Gazette

Migrating snow geese inhabit marshes of Virginia Beach, now a Federal game preserve.

wild pigeon. The last buffalo recorded in Virginia was killed in 1804, and the species was nearly exterminated across the land in the next century. William Byrd II in the eighteenth century described the buffalo as "an animal with a hump on its back, of an enormous and terrible size, has long curly hair, from which the Indians make many things and Europeans [make] mattresses."

Naturalists estimate 20 million of the big brutes lived in the West in 1850, reduced by 1890 to 551. Game laws and national parks have since raised the buffalo count to many thousands, mostly in the West.

Wild pigeons, also called passenger pigeons, which were a favorite game of early Americans, have been wiped out totally. But two other endangered species have revived under protection laws. One is the beaver, whose pelts were once valued for men's hats, and the other is the wild turkey, now protected by a limited season. A lively beaver dam may be seen on the Chickahominy River.

Peninsula suburbs increasingly attract deer, raccoons, squirrels and song birds, which used to feed on crops that are no longer planted. Many householders begrudge them their expensive backyard azaleas, tulips and lettuce, but Audubon societies oppose the use of poisons and animal traps. It's becoming an issue everywhere.

As for Bill Snyder, he's on the side of the animals.

56. *Life on a Scallop Boat*

HOW WOULD YOU LIKE to spend two weeks in a 90-foot trawler 200 miles off the Atlantic coast, tossing about in the wintry Atlantic?

Well, that's an everyday experience for scallop fishermen on the 22 fishing boats of the Seaford Scallop Company, which operates out of Back Creek in York County, close to York River. They bring back a big share of the many million pounds of scallops caught yearly by trawlers from Hampton, Newport News, Seaford, and elsewhere in Tidewater.

The 15-year-old Seaford company has helped make sea scallops (they're big scallops, as opposed to smaller bay scallops) one of the more profitable Virginia catches. Virginia scallop sales bring fishermen some $30 million in good years, rivalling income from the Chesapeake blue crab.

Most Virginia scallop boats are based close to Hampton roads, so they can easily reach the beds of hard-shelled scallops that lie along the Atlantic shelf. Illegally small scallops must be thrown back in the sea to mature. The 50-odd Virginia-based scallop boats hotly compete to find new scallop beds before others get there.

Now and then a scalloper will dredge up a torpedo left over from German U-boat warfare in the Atlantic during World War II. Most of them are duds, but crews treat them gingerly. After all, one could explode.

I learned a bit about scallops from Bill Wells (William Wells III, to be formal), who operates

VIMS photo by William DuPaul

Ocean scallops resemble clams, but only part of their flesh inside is edible.

VIMS photo by William DuPaul

A scallop trawler fishes in deep water off the Atlantic, hauling in shellfish in its chain bag.

from Seaford with his father and V.J. O'Neal. Their boats scour the Atlantic shelf all year, bringing home millions of dollars in scallops and other seafoods. After all, ocean scallops retail for around $5 a pound, despite increasing competition from Oriental and European producers.

Much of the Seaford scallop catch is purchased by Red Lobster restaurants, Chesapeake Bay Seafood Houses, and wholesalers as far west as California. After all, low calorie scallops are popular right now with yuppies and other weight-watchers.

I met Bill Wells in his dock house office on Seaford's tiny waterfront. There he keeps in touch by radio with his boats at sea, and there he works with repairmen, refrigeration engineers, and the public at his dockside office. The 300-employee firm has grown since Wells and his father moved to Virginia from Key West in 1979, after shrimping declined there.

Scallop fishing is an offshore enterprise, governed by Federal laws, rather than a Chesapeake Bay activity like most fishing, governed by Virginia and Maryland regulations. "Our nation got into offshore fishing in 1976," Wells tells me, "when the United States asserted control of all fisheries for 200 miles off the North American coastline. The Magnuson Act passed by Congress in that year stated that the United States could deny foreign ships' requests to fish our territorial waters. The purpose was to de-emphasize foreign fishing in American waters and to promote American fishing."

As a result, fewer Eastern European and Oriental trawlers now invade United States waters. No foreign ships are known to be fishing for scallops at present in the near Atlantic.

Wells' trawlers, costing about $550,000 each,

are deep-draft vessels with capacious below-deck refrigerators to store the catch until the boat returns to Seaford to discharge cargo. The sturdy ships are built to operate northward to New England's Georges Bank, often in heavy seas. In prolonged bad weather they return to port without a full catch.

"None of our captains has less than three years' sea-going experience, and every vessel has the latest navigational and communications gear," Wells says. This includes two radios, radar, fathometer, LORAN, and other devices.

Running a scallop trawler requires skill and knowledge. One Seaford trawler skipper has a degree in chemical engineering. Another completed pre-medical education before going to sea. Once at sea, the trawler hunts for scallops by dragging his powerful dredge with its metal "chain bag" over the ocean floor to scoop up the large clam-shaped scallops, each about three and a half inches wide.

Once the ship locates a bed, it concentrates and pulls up its dredge only long enough to empty the chain bag every 35 minutes or so. Then the crew quickly dumps the net's harvest of scallops and cuts out the large white muscle—the "scallop"—in each shell, throwing the shells back into the sea.

Each of the eleven-member crew stands a six-hour watch, working constantly to drag the dredge, unload it, and cut up the catch for refrigeration. Work continues all night around the clock. The vessel usually stays at sea two weeks.

Scallop dredges often bring up flounder, monkfish, squid, ocean quahogs, and clams. This incidental catch, called "shack," is sold to wholesalers in home port.

On the waterfront at Seaford facing his office, Bill Wells pointed to a docked trawler whose engine problem had forced it back home after eight days at sea. It had caught about 5,000 pound of scallops plus 1,200 pounds of flounder and 200 pounds of monkfish. Of the catch, the crew gets 60 percent, less expenses, while the owner gets 40 percent, less expenses. A good catch can yield a rich reward.

VIMS photo by William DuPaul

Huge chain bag is scraped over ocean floor by trawler to bring up scallops and deepwater fish.

Like all fishing, scalloping is an up-and-down business. "We seem to run in ten-year cycles," Wells says. "This year we appear to be overfished again, as we were in 1981. The last really good year was 1976."

Though scallop catches are declining, marine biologists report good spawning of the shellfish in recent years. It takes three years to produce scallops big enough to harvest. That means no fewer than 36 scallops to the pound. "Our small industry is moving rapidly into the high-tech twentieth century," Wells says. "We're being revolutionized by better techniques."

57. *Gloucester's Golden Age*

TO GLOUCESTER'S wealthy landowners of 60 years ago, Hampton and Newport News, across the York, seemed "declassé," says Katherine Withers Hamilton of Gloucester.

The lifelong Gloucester resident visited the Peninsula before World War I to attend performances at the Newport News Academy of Music that her father, Alfred Withers, had built on Washington Avenue in 1897 to provide entertainment for the infant town. But rural Gloucester is where she wants to be.

"We spent a week in Newport News in the early 1900s," she recalls, "and saw Joseph Jefferson play his famous role, 'Rip Van Winkle'."

Despite such touring road shows, however, the Academy lost money and was sold by Withers to the Klaw and Erlanger theatrical chain. It was later resold and torn down in the 1930s to give way to the Paramount movie theater, now razed.

Born at Severnby plantation in 1905, Katherine Withers married Philip Wellford Hamilton of Petersburg. Between them, they were related to many Gloucester families. "There were lots of charming eccentrics in those days," she recalls. "In fact, Gloucester was much nicer then than after they built the bridge across the York."

An outspoken 98-year-old lady of strong opinions, Katherine Hamilton has seen nearly all her contemporaries die. Though partly crippled, she enjoys her family and reads widely. An avid gardener, she raises flowers and vegetables in waist-high boxes. A son and daughter-in-law live next door to her in Severnby's Victorian waterfront house, and two servants wait on her.

Books line the walls in Mrs. Hamilton's house, and a pet kitten reposes by the hearth. Antique furnishings and oil portraits reflect the wealth of forebears: The Withers of Binghampton, New York; the Morrises of Philadelphia; the Hamiltons of Petersburg; and the Pages and Vandegrifts and others of Gloucester's families.

Of them all, Mrs. Hamilton would like most to be her father. "He sat in a big chair all day and read," she says, purring approval. "He was the most cultivated man I ever knew. He read everything, even though he stopped school at 16."

Part of her admiration derives from her father's independent mind. He ran away from his parents' house, worked his way to England, and enlisted in the British army to fight the Fuzzy-Wuzzies in the Second Sudan campaign. He took part in the battles of El Teb and Tamai, being

Mrs. Katherine Hamilton, 98, with her cousin Cecil Page on sofa from family plantation, Rosewell.

wounded and left for dead on one battlefield.

"He had to buy his way out of the British army," his daughter recalls, but he served in the U. S. Army a few years later in World War I. However, he died after the 1918 Armistice without having gotten overseas.

Fortunately, Alfred Withers inherited more than a million dollars and "lived like an English squire," his daughter recalls. He married Katherine Page Vandegrift of Gloucester, and they had a son, who was killed while diving into a swimming pool, plus several daughters. Besides Mrs. Hamilton, they are Mrs. Grafton Dulany Addison of Richmond and Mrs. Bruce Warden of Washington, D.C.

A devotee of the stage, Alfred Withers in his best years bought a yacht from actor Richard Mansfield. He was also interested in horse racing like his uncle, Dunham Withers, for whom the Withers Mile at New York's Belmont track is named. "Mother was a great fox hunter in the days when Gloucester hunted," Mrs. Hamilton adds.

Once in a Hampton drugstore during World War I, her father heard a man say, "All British soldiers are cowards." "My father was so incensed he knocked the man down," she says proudly.

The Newport News shipbuilding boom in 1897-98 during the Spanish-American War, encouraged Alfred Withers to buy Washington Avenue land in 1897 and to spend $100,000 building the European-style academy of music. A Gloucester-born architect, Charles Dimmock, who had designed the Withers' house, Severnby, designed the academy.

On the quiet Gloucester waterfront, away from the traffic on booming Route 17, Katherine Hamilton lives much as her ancestors have lived. Nearby lies Eagle Point plantation, once owned by the Withers family, and Warner Hall, rebuilt on the site of Augustine Warner's colonial mansion. "Out here in the country, everybody lives in his private world," she exults.

Thinking over her life, Katherine Hamilton is grateful for Gloucester in horse-and-buggy days. "It was much nicer before it attracted real estate developers," she declares. "It was a self-contained county, like English rural society. Now it's cosmopolitan."

In earlier days, the river steamer *Mobjack* linked the Gloucester peninsula with Old Point and Norfolk, she recalls. "It was a ritual for Gloucester folk to drive down to the dock and meet the boat. At Roane's Wharf, which served us, every family had its own hitching post. The artist, Roland Clark, would sail over in his boat. Everybody talked till the *Mobjack* arrived."

"Captain Caffee was master of the *Mobjack,*" she continues, "and his wife would go to Norfolk and buy household necessities for all her Gloucester neighbors." The *Mobjack* brought to Gloucester large cakes of ice in burlap from Norfolk, plus much other cargo.

One of her father's friends was novelist Thomas Dixon, who wrote *The Clansman,* which was made into the movie, "The Birth of a Nation." Dixon lived awhile on the North River at Elmington, which he renamed Dixondale. He called Gloucester "the land of the life worth living."

Much as she deplores Gloucester's growth, Katherine Hamilton is thankful for her long and eventful life. "I've had a happy time," she says. "I've been fortunate." Surrounded by family, dogs, cats and books, she stays as far away as possible from the booming corridor of Gloucester's Route 17. In rural Gloucester she has found the life worth living.

Daily Press

Daffodils, blooming here at Gloucester Courthouse, are widely sold as bulbs and flowers.

58. *Forgotten Counties, New Cities*

A LOT OF HISTORIC buildings have perished on the Peninsula since Jamestown was settled in 1607. Hampton was the worst hit, for it was burned by the British in 1813 and again by its own Confederate defenders in 1861. Otherwise its downtown today might look much like what's been preserved of Williamsburg or Yorktown. From all accounts, it was a charming seaport village, what with its Rose and Crown Tavern, its Little England and Little Scotland plantations, and on Hampton Creek a few waterside windmills to grind local corn and wheat.

Little England on Hampton Creek was the home of Hampton's wealthy Balfour family, who intermarried with the Blairs of Williamsburg. Handsome Balfour portraits survive in Richmond at the Virginia Historical Society.

Their onetime plantation house stood near the former Queen Street Bridge fronting a deep water dock. British ships called there, creating some confusion among subsequent historians with the other Little England plantation, owned by the Perrin family on the York River at Sarah's Creek. (The latter fortunately survives.)

Another Hampton plantation was Celey's, once on Chesapeake Avenue near Salter's Creek. It was at various times the home of the Celey, Wilson and Cary families. The house survived the Civil War, but then was razed.

Old Point was fortified early because of its strategic site, fronting the Virginia capes across Hampton Roads and the bay. Long gone, however, is Fort Algernon, built there beginning about 1610 to guard the bay. It was later rebuilt as Fort

Virginia Gazette

Yorktown's Main Street has lost post-Civil War poverty and is restored by Park Service.

Hampton's homes were burned by Confederate owners in August 1861 to prevent falling into Union hands.

George by the Barron family, who kept watch against pirates and other enemies. A descendent of that family, Commodore James Barron, dueled and killed Commodore Stephen Decatur in 1820. In the 1820s, Fort Monroe replaced tiny Fort George, becoming a U.S. Army coastal defense.

A wealth of old buildings has come and gone at Old Point since then, including the long-famous Hotel Hygeia and the first Hotel Chamberlin, which burned in 1920 and was replaced by the present Chamberlin in 1928.

Among early Hampton plantations now gone are Chesterville, near Langley Field, where George Wythe was born in 1726, and Roseland Manor near Phoebus, where lived the nineteenth-century hotelier, Harrison Phoebus, who made the Hygeia into a popular spa and resort hotel. Nearby stood the Union's Chesapeake Hospital in the Civil War, later to become the center of the present veteran's facility. The old building no longer stands.

In suburban York County, between Yorktown and Hampton, once stood Hampton Parish Church of York County, which in 1707 was combined with the larger York Parish at Yorktown.

The foundations of Yorkhampton's early church, which had been created under the ministry of the Reverend George Keith in 1635, survive in eastern York, near the foundations of the Halfway House inn, which once served Peninsula travelers. On the James River, all of the half-dozen pre-Civil War plantation houses and the tiny Episcopal church once on Mulberry Island have long since disappeared. The area was absorbed by Fort Eustis as a gunnery range in World War I.

Yorktown suffered great losses in 1781, when George Washington and Comte de Rochambeau attacked Lord Cornwallis's British forces there in the climactic battle of the Revolutionary War. The beautiful houses of the Amblers and the Lightfoots, two of the town's leading merchants, were so badly damaged that they were never repaired.

On the James River shore of the Peninsula, several plantation houses have disappeared. One is Greenspring near Jamestown, where the Ludwell family and later their Ludwell-Lee descendants lived. On the James near the Chickahominy River once stood Teddington, the big frame house of the once-prosperous Lightfoot family, which was destroyed by fire early this century.

Among the few industries of the Peninsula in

colonial times were corn and wheat mills. Among those in eighteenth and nineteenth century James City County which have disappeared are Ludwell's Mill (later Jones' Mill) at Williamsburg, Kennon's (later Coleman's) near Jamestown and Waller Mill near the present Williamsburg reservoir.

In nearby York are the remains or Custis' Mill, researched by Colonial Williamsburg, and in the western end of Newport News are the mill ponds of Harwood's and of Young's mills, the latter owned by the Young family of Denbigh plantation.

These are only a few of the colonial landmarks that have disappeared on the Peninsula. They give archaeologists a lot to investigate, along with the earlier Indian sites which dot this historic heart of America.

Few Peninsula residents remember Elizabeth City and Warwick counties, which were consolidated in the 1950s into Hampton and Newport News, respectively. But they were historic counties, both among the first eight shires created by the Virginia settlers in 1634.

Six of the first eight Virginia shires or counties were cut from the Peninsula: James City, Charles City, Warwick River (later simply Warwick), Henrico, Elizabeth City and Charles River (renamed York). The two others were Warrosquyoake, renamed Isle of Wight, and Accomack on the Eastern Shore. Except for Elizabeth City and Warwick, all the others survive, although the boundaries of most have been changed due to the creation of new counties and annexation by cities.

Warwick and Elizabeth City were Virginia's smallest counties. Warwick contained 65 square miles and Elizabeth City 51 square miles.

Thomas Jefferson once complained that Warwick County was over-represented in the House of Burgesses because it had two delegates, the same as other counties more populous than Warwick. Warwick had only about 2,000 residents until the Chesapeake & Ohio Railway came down the Peninsula to Newport News in 1881, attracting newcomers. Elizabeth City was more prominent than Warwick because the port of Hampton served trans-Atlantic ships and Chesapeake Bay schooners hauling tobacco, corn, seafood, and timber. Hampton's shipping declined after the Civil War when deeper-draft steamers replaced sailing ships. In the early 1900s, Hampton boasted daily steamboat service to Norfolk, Old Point, and other Hampton Roads' localities. Old Point and Fort Monroe added to Elizabeth City County's fame and population.

Early Elizabeth City records include such family names as Kirby, Westwood, Balfour, Wythe, Hunter, Sclater, Peek, Fosque, Marrow, Holt, Mallory, Phillips and Sinclair. Among early Warwick families were Carys, Blounts, Roscows, Garrows, Mallicottes, Curtises, Harwoods and Woodwards. Some of the names persist.

Warwick County tried to create a port in 1680, when the Virginia Assembly chose 50 acres of Samuel Mathews' Denbigh Plantation, on Warwick River, as the site of Warwick Town. By 1690 a courthouse and jail were erected there and used until about 1790. But Warwick Town was too far from the beaten path, and in 1809 the county seat was moved to Stoney Run along the cart path which then connected Williamsburg and Newport News Point.

In 1810 a three-room Warwick Courthouse was built there, plus an office and a jail. Drawings made during the Civil War show this courthouse, used early in the war as a bivouac area by Confederates. In 1862, Federal soldiers camped there and stole county record books, which remain missing. During Reconstruction, court sessions were held by Federal officers of the Freedmen's Bureau.

After the C&O tracks in 1881 were laid down the Peninsula to Newport News, the seat of Warwick County was moved to Newport News, which then became the populous end of the county. A new Warwick County courthouse was built at 25th Street and Lafayette (later renamed Huntington) Avenue. When, in 1896, Newport News was carved out of Warwick and became a city, the county court site was moved back to its

Virginia Gazette

Marshal Petain, President and Mrs. Hoover, Gen. Pershing, and Senator Hiram Bingham were at 1931 York Sesquicentennial.

previous site at Stoney Run. There the old building remains.

The city took over the courthouse at 25th Street, and sessions there were immortalized in the 1900s by Walter Kelly, an Irish Catholic bartender from Pennsylvania, who in his spare time frequented the hilarious police court of Judge J. D. G. (John Douglas Gordon) Brown. Kelly originated a vaudeville monologue, "The Virginian Judge," and after he retired to Hollywood wrote his autobiography. In it he recalled:

> On my maiden visit to this classic Temple of Justice I found a motley crowd, male and female, with bandaged hands and bleary eyes, awaited the decrees of Judge Brown. Around the big fireless stove sprawled an ominous-looking pack of liver-colored bloodhounds belonging to the sheriff, for use in his frequent manhunts. The jailer stood at the pen door, dangling an eight-inch ring of half-pound keys, and at a desk adjoining the judge's bench sat a prematurely bald clerk, scanning the docket. Over all hung the stench and acrid odor of wet dogs and hot bodies.

Warwick County built a new jail in 1899. It was the practice of the Warwick jailer to permit inmates to leave the lockup to cut the courthouse grass or to walk to the nearby creek and fish for their supper. More dangerous Warwick criminals were kept in the Hampton jail.

The post-World War II growth of the Peninsula led to consolidation moves which eliminated the ancient counties of Elizabeth City and Warwick. The consolidation of Hampton, Phoebus and Elizabeth City County became effective July 1, 1952. Consolidation of Warwick, then a city, and Newport News, became effective July 1, 1958.

Attempts to consolidate Hampton and Newport News failed. Hampton now has more than 126,000 people and Newport News more than 161,000. That makes Newport News Virginia's fourth most populous city, after Virginia Beach, Norfolk and Richmond. Hampton is sixth.

59. *World Fame of the Blue Crab*

SUMMER is crabbing season in the Chesapeake Bay, and that's my time of year. As the bay warms in April, millions of hard crabs that buried themselves in the soft mud in the fall begin to dig out and flood the creeks and rivers again. They grow and reproduce all summer, only to return to their hideaway when winter comes.

I've been fascinated by the crab's life cycle since I began catching them in the James River at Newport News when I was a boy in the 1920s. It is the most valuable of all marine species in the Chesapeake, bring watermen some $35 million wholesale at dockside. The blue crab is to Virginia and Maryland what the lobster is to Maine.

But are we catching too many, as we've done with rockfish, shad, herring and perch? As other species decline, more watermen are going after crabs. The invention of the crab pot by the late B.F. Lewis of Harryhogan in the later 1920s has increased the catch.

Once sold for $4 or $5 a pound, picked from its shell, crabmeat is becoming as expensive as lobster.

You may not consider the Chesapeake Bay blue crab exotic, but I do. Until recently, its lifespan has been unknown to most laymen. Caught on a line baited with meat, it snaps at you with claws that can inflict severe pain. Its blue-green

Virginia Division of Tourism

On Tangier Island in the bay waterman nets soft crabs that have busted overnight in his crab float.

Crab pot fisherman empties overnight catch from wire crab pot into baskets for market.

shell, which changes subtly with its age and habitat, is a masterpiece of camouflage. A bright contrast is the lipstick red of its claws, especially the females.

No wonder William Warner called his account of the Chesapeake's favorite shellfish *Beautiful Swimmers*. Warner dramatized the crab's life cycle to make readers aware of the need for more restraint in catching them, but it didn't help much.

Virginia and Maryland estimate that commercial fishermen catch nearly a million pounds of crabs a year. But there's no way of telling how many more pounds are caught by recreational crabbers, like me, who under Virginia law can operate one crab pot each. An expert at the Virginia Institute of Marine Science says recreational crabbers' catch may equal that of commercial crabbers, who can use an unlimited number of pots.

We Gloucester folk hang our crab pots from our community pier on the York at Gloucester Point, baiting them with dead fish. Most of us pull them up every morning, finding up to 10 or 12 crabs in each. Offshore, from shoal water to the York channel, are hundreds of commercial crab pots, each marked by a float. Each morning I watch the commercial crabbers go out by boat and harvest their pots, replacing the bait.

Pleasure boaters in Chesapeake rivers like the York deplore the crab pots, which make navigation difficult. Sometimes water skiers run afoul of crab pot lines.

The annual crab catch varies, depending on

water conditions the preceding year, which influence the survival rate of crabs.

Thus far, crab-catch laws remain liberal, though VIMS and other biologists carefully monitor crab reproduction and catches. Laws are getting tighter.

In recent years Chesapeake crabbers have begun to ship soft crabs to Japan, Hong Kong and other Oriental markets. The iced crabs are carefully arranged on flats and flown from Baltimore and Washington.

Most of today's soft crabs are sold by watermen who maintain soft crab floats in which "peelers" are kept until they molt out of their hard shells into a soft one. As the soft shell—mostly made of chitin, the substance found in fingernails—hardens in 72 hours, the soft crabs must be taken from saltwater soon after molting and prepared for shipment.

I know several soft crab producers around Gloucester Point. They obtain peelers from shoal water in low tide or by purchase from commercial crab pot operators and put them in floats or pounds to let them "peel" or "bust" out of their hard shells. Soft crabs usually bring about $1 apiece in medium size and $2 for "main channelers."

Virginia's Tangier Island in Chesapeake Bay is called the soft crab capital of the world because of the many crustaceans netted from its crab floats and sent by air express to the Orient and across the nation. Soft crabs are a cherished delicacy in Japan, where they are called "crabs of the moonlight sea" because they shed in greatest numbers during the full moon.

Although the Chesapeake Bay blue crab is caught southward from the Chesapeake to Florida and the Gulf Coast, about 95 percent of all those harvested soft are caught in Virginia.

Beside crab pots and baited handlines, crabs are caught in dip nets by waders at low tide or in wire traps suspended from piers and baited with chicken or fish. Commercial crabbers also catch them on trotlines, in pound traps built along deepwater shorelines, and in dredges—the latter used in winter to suck up crabs buried underwater. But crabs in winter are poor.

The crab cycle begins when a mature male mates with a female preparing to molt. He carries her underneath him for two or three days prior to her molting, to guard her from predators. The fertilized female grows a sponge containing thousands of minuscule eggs, from which develop tiny zoea, or larvae. After several larval stages, the tiny crab takes shape. It grows by molting every three to five days. As the crab approaches maturity, it molts about every 20 to 50 days.

At Gloucester, I find the crabs at their greatest abundance in August and September, when they have grown big. They're said to molt or "bust" chiefly at full moons, especially in August.

If you haven't tried crabbing—either by dipnet, handline, wire trap or crab pot—do so.

Virginia Tourism Development Group

The blue crab remains abundant in Chesapeake despite heavy annual catches.

Bald eagles were once endangered in Virginia but are slowly increasing.

Virginia Gazette

60. *The Return of the Eagle*

EVER SINCE the bald eagle became the national emblem by vote of Congress in 1782, the big bird has enjoyed a special mystique. It came as a surprise, therefore, to realize that the noble predator lives in Tidewater and feeds off the fish it finds in creeks and rivers.

College of William and Mary

William and Mary biologist Mitchell Byrd says bald eagles are increasing along Virginia waterways.

A specialist in eagles is Mitchell Byrd, chancellor professor of biology at the College of William and Mary. Byrd works with state game and fisheries officials on problems relating to endangered species, especially the bald eagle. (It's not really bald but white-headed and white-tailed, with brown body features.)

Actually, the bald eagle is found in all parts of North America near water, with a northern species in Canada slightly larger than the southern found down here.

As leader of a United States Fish and Wildlife Bald Eagle Recovery Team, Byrd spends hundreds of hours annually flying over the Chesapeake Bay watershed with binoculars looking for bald eagles.

He's encouraged that nesting eagles are increasing in Tidewater, thanks to the government's prohibition of DDT in insecticides. It was the DDT—condemned by Rachel Carson in her 1962 book, *Silent Spring*—that entered the food chain and weakened the shells of eagle eggs so that they broke easily while in the nest.

This year the news is better. "Consider my mid-winter flyover of the Rappahannock River," Byrd recently reported. "I counted 97 eagles on a two-mile stretch of river front, 36 in one small

Two young eagles wait at their nest in a Virginia pine to be fed by their scavenging parents.

area alone. Considering that only 65 breeding pairs were found in all of the Chesapeake Bay region in 1977, the wintering population along this one tributary of the bay is remarkable."

Byrd is heartened that Americans are aware at last of environmental threats and are doing something about them.

But the news isn't all good. "The chilling part came as I saw the ever-growing number of homes, roads, parking lots and shopping centers creeping toward eagle nesting and roosting sites," Byrd reports. "As more homes, roads and shopping centers are built, the bald eagles which use the area in both winter and summer, will find their habitat severely reduced."

The dilemma remains: as more waterfront land is developed, more eagles will flee Tidewater in search of wilderness.

Byrd therefore recommends that the U.S. Fish and Wildlife Service reconsider its current proposal to downgrade the bald eagle from "endangered" to "threatened" under the Endangered Species Act of 1973.

"Instead of downgrading the status of the bald eagle, we should be vigorously working toward preserving its habitat," Byrd believes. "Recent projections estimate 2 million more people will be living in the bay's basin by the year 2020. While Maryland has worked to restrict shoreline development, the federal government and the state of Virginia have done little to establish significant habitat areas."

If you have traveled Peninsula waterways in recent years, you may have seen nesting eagles. I saw some recently on a trip up the swampy Chickahominy River. I saw others in the tall pines along Queen's Creek, a picturesque York County tributary of the York.

Thus far, both Queen's Creek and the Chickahominy have remained relatively undeveloped. But biologists know the eagle is a loner and moves away when man comes close. That's happened on the Lower Peninsula, where people have taken over the waterfront.

Benjamin Franklin, you remember, suggested we make the turkey our American emblem because it is peculiarly North American. Franklin knew that the eagle had been the emblem of one of the Ptolemies of Egypt and was borne on the standards of the Roman armies and of

Napoleon's troops in his European battles.

But Congress was wise to choose the solitary bird with the fierce eye and the lethal beak and talons. It warns marauders to stay away.

The eagle is a member of the hawk family and is thought to mate for life—a good example for Americans. It builds its nest of twigs and sticks high up near some waterway, and adds to it year after year. A nesting pair usually produce two young, which do not develop adult markings until their third year, when they leave parental protection and fly off to seek their own mates and territories.

The ancients believed eagles sometimes carried off small children as prey, but that's untrue. Despite the legend of Ganymede, the biggest eagle can lift no more than eight pounds. It usually prefers its prey dead, sometimes robbing ospreys of their catch.

The bald eagle is found in all states of the union except Hawaii. National inventories kept by the United States Fish and Wildlife Service show the species declined to only 417 nesting pairs in the lower 48 states in 1963. However, a recent survey showed a population of 3,747 pairs. Clearly the eagles are increasing.

Researchers credit the comeback largely to the banning of DDT. In some places, power lines that had electrocuted the birds were redesigned.

The eagle was named the national bird in 1782 when the Founding Fathers overrode Benjamin Franklin's proposal to designate the turkey. It is called bald eagle because its white head feathers give that impression. The bird has a reputation for fierceness but is actually rather timid.

Flying around over Tidewater, biologist Byrd worries about the growth of houses and docks along once-isolated streams. "If we do not take action to preserve the nesting and feeding areas of our nation's bird," he warns, "the bald eagle population will once again likely decline, with the result that it will need to be placed back on the endangered species list."

He adds: "And if we have subsequently destroyed the wild areas in which they live and feed, it will be far more difficult—perhaps impossible—to bring the eagles back from the edge a second time."

I hope Americans will take this warning to heart.

Daily Press

This mature eagle is one of about 125 counted on Prince George County shoreline of the James.

Acknowledgements

I am grateful to the Newport News *Daily Press* for its cooperation in the publication of this book, made up largely of columns I have written for that paper. I especially thank editor Jack Davis, editorial page editor Will Molineux, and librarians Nancy Coram and Melissa Simpson, the latter two assisting with illustrations. At the Swem Library of the College of William and Mary I thank Hope Yelich of the reference department. Also at the college I received help from Dean Olson of publications and Professor Mitchell Byrd of the biology faculty. At *The Virginia Gazette* I thank publisher and editor Bill O'Donovan and managing editor Susan Bruno for their release of pictures. For information on Fort Eustis and the early Peninsula, I am indebted to Dick Ivey of the Fort Eustis Historical Society. Wilford Kale and the Virginia Marine Resources Commission were most helpful. I am grateful to Mary Keeling of the Colonial Williamsburg Foundation audiovisual library; to naturalist Bill Snyder of James City County; to Ben McCary of Williamsburg for information on early Virginia Indians; to the Union Camp Corporation of Franklin for information on Dismal Swamp; to Betsy Fleet of King William County for biographical data on Henry Fleete; to Weymouth Crumpler of Newport News for background on the first plane takeoff in history from a Navy ship; and to Martin Gracey of Newport News for information on the Schneider Cup races in Hampton Roads in 1926. I thank Maurice Duke of Virginia Commonwealth University for information and photographs relating to the lost village of Queenstown in Lancaster County; Owen Phillips of Newport News for material on his ancestor, Thomas Phillips, who defied the Union naval blockade in the Civil War; and Martha Stewart of the Mariners' Museum in Newport News, who provided me with a list of maritime and naval museums on the Atlantic Coast. My daughter, Sarah Rouse Sheehan, kindly supplied photographs from the Library of Congress, where she works. Illustrations are credited individually, beneath each picture, but I would like to thank especially the Colonial Williamsburg Foundation, the Mariners' Museum, the Virginia State Library, the Maryland Historical Society, the Casemate Museum at Fort Monroe, the Fort Eustis Museum, Lt. Col. Philip Hamilton of Gloucester, Lt. Col. Cecil Page of Gloucester, Mrs. Anne Darling Tormey of Hampton, the Virginia Chamber of Commerce, Flowerdieu Hundred Foundation, Lawrence Loftin, Jr., the Virginia Departments of Agriculture and of Economic Development, and the Virginia Division of Tourism.

Bibliography

Most of the information in this book was obtained by interview with living persons, but a few chapters are based wholly or partly on the following publications:

Beyer, Edward: *Album of Virginia;* Richmond, 1858.

Dixon, Thomas, Jr.: *The Life Worth Living;* Doubleday, 1905.

Fleet, Betsy: *Henry Fleete: Pioneer, Explorer, Trader, Planter, Legislator, Justice, and Peacemaker;* Whittet and Shepperson, 1989.

Green, Bennett: *A Word-Book of Virginia Folk-Speech;* W. E. Jones, 1899.

Guinness, Alec: *Blessings in Disguise;* Knopf, 1985.

Lossing, Benson: *A Pictorial Field-Book of the War of 1812;* Harper and Brothers, 1869.

Middleton, Pierce: *Tobacco Coast;* Mariners' Museum, 1953.

Rouse, Parke, Jr.: *The Timber Tycoons: The Camp Families of Virginia and Florida and Their Empire, 1887, 1987;* Southampton County Historical Society, 1988.

Stanard, William G., *Notes on a Journey on the James;* Association for the Preservation of Virginia Antiquities, 1913.

Index

A History of the Dividing Line, 25
A Journey in the Seaboard Slave States, 28
A Word-Book of Virginia Folk-Speech, 149–151
Aberdeen, 32
Abbott, Stanley, 120
Abolitionists, 78
Accomac, ship, 84
Accomack County, 167–169
Acosta, Bert, 100
Acree, David, 80, 133
Adams, John Quincy, 89
Addison, Mrs. Grafton, 179
Aeronautical Chronology, 112
Africa, 15
Afrika Corps, 154
Air & Space Magazine, 113
Air Combat Command, 105
Alaska, 3
Albemarle Hall Hotel, 152
Albemarle Sound, 25, 27, 29
Alexandria, 157–160
Algonquin Indians, 4
Allen family, 140
Allston, Mass., 115
American Revolution, 17–19, 26, 32–34
Ampthill plantation, 102
Anacostan Indians, 7
Andrews, Frank, 122
Anglican Church, 36
Annapolis, 123
Appomattox Manor plantation, 102–103

Archer's Hope, 11, 102
Arctic pole, 4
Ariel, ship, 74, 75, 101–103
Armstrong, John, 53
Army Corps of Engineers, 24–29, 55–56
Army of the Potomac, 55–56
Army Transportation Command, 68–70
Arnold, Hap, 114, 122
Ashby, Turner, 162
Ashe, William, 106–108
Asia, 3
Assignation houseboats, 125
Association for the Preservation of Virginia Antiquities, 94–96, 101–103
Atlantic Coast, 43
Austin, Herbert, 164
Ayres, B. Drummond, 80, 81
Azores, 33

Back Creek, 175
Bacon, Anthony, 26
Bacon, Nathaniel, Jr., 44–46, 17
Bacon's Castle, 140
Bacon's Rebellion, 5, 25
Bailey, Charles W., 68–70
'Bailey's Bungalow,' 69
Baldwin, Thomas Scott, 100
Ball, Mary, 11
Ball, William, 11
Ballard Street, Yorktown, 106
Ball's Point, 11
Baltimore, 147–148

Baltimore & Ohio Railway, 147
Baptists, 46
Barbour, James, 51–53
Barney, Edward E., 101
Barron, James, 182
Barthelmess, Richard, 100
Bassett Hall, 27
Bath, N.C., 16
Battery Park, 84
Battle of Fair Oaks, 66–67
Bay Shore Hotel Company, 85
Beach bathing, 119–121
Beautiful Swimmers, 186
Beavers, 174
Benjamin Harrison Bridge, 4
Bennett, Gordon, 112
Bering Strait, 3
Berkeley plantation, 74, 102–103
  See also Harrison's Landing
Berkeley, Sir William, 5
Beckwith, Sir Sydney, 51–53
Boston, 115–118
Bottom fishing, 138
Boulevard at Hampton, 119
Bowers, Dudie, 86
Bozarth, W. A., 108
Brandon plantation, 102–103
Braxton, Carter, 116
Brazil, 122
Bridges and tunnels, 167–169
Bristol, England, 16, 34
British army, 17–19, 27, 51–53
British navy, 54–56
Broadribb, William, 36
Broadwater, John, 41–44

193

Brooks, Archie, 108
Brown, J.D.G., 184
Bruton Parish Church, 38, 107
Bryce, Lord, 94
Buckroe Beach, 85, 87, 120–121
Buckroe plantation, 85
Buffalo, 174
Buggs Island Dam, 3
Bull's Head Tavern, 108
Burr, Aaron, 162
Burwell, Robert C., 26
Burwell's Bay, 102
Busch Gardens, 86
Bush, George, 65
Byrd, Harry, Sr., 117
Byrd, Mitchell, 186–190
Byrd, Richard E., 100
Byrd, William, II, 11, 23–29

Calhoun, John C., 54–56, 154
Calvert, George, 7
Camp brothers, Franklin, 23–29
Camp Hill, 137
Camp Manufacturing Company, 29
Camp, William Nelson, 24
Camp Patrick Henry, 155–156
Camp Peary, 121
Camp Stuart, 100
Canary Islands, 33
Cape Charles, 5, 32–34, 167–169
Cape Hatteras, 72
Cape Henry, 20, 22, 32–34, 110
Captain Caffee, 180
Carbon radiation, 3
Careless Point, 5
Caribbean, 15, 16, 34
Carlstrom, Victor, 100
Carson, Rachel, 29, 188
Carter, Robert 'King,' 11
Carter's Grove, 11, 38, 79, 101
Casey, Louis S., 100
Casino grounds, Newport News, 82–84, 119
Castle Calhoun, 54–56
Castle, Vernon, 100
Cedar Lane plantation, 139
Celey's plantation, 50, 161–162
Chamberlin Hotel, 78, 181–182
Chambers, Washington, 99
Chapman, Elizabeth,
Charles City County, 6, 58, 66, 73–75, 89
Chasseurs Britanniques, 53
Cheatham Annex, 121
Chesapeake Avenue, Hampton, 50

Chesapeake Bay, 8, 13, 16, 45–47, 104–105
Chesapeake Bay Magazine, 167–169
Chesapeake, city of, 26
Chesapeake Hospital, 182
Chesterville plantation, 182
Chevalier, Godfrey, 110–111
Clinton, Sir Henry, 17–19
Chewning, Alpheus J., 153
Chinn's Ordinary, 162
Chickahominy River, 102–103
Chickahominy Swamp, 66–67
Chowning's Tavern, 163
Christ Church, Alexandria, 157
Christiana Campbell's Tavern, 163
Churchill, William, 22
Chiles, Edward, 85
Civil War, 17, 24, 40, 61–64, 80, 162, 181–183
Civil War blockade, 71
Claiborne, William C., 7, 8, 10
Claremont Manor plantation, 14, 140
Clark, Mark, 155
Clark, Roland, 180
Clarksville, 3
Clay, Henry, 58, 162
Claremont, ship, 74
Clovis, New Mexico, 3
Clovis points, 3
Coast Aeronautical Station, 104–105
Coast Guard, 46–47
Coast Guard Reserve Training Center, 20–22
Cockburn, Sir George, 49–50
Cocke, Duncan, 37
Cocke, Preston, 108
Cofer, John I., Jr., 84
Cohen, Sammy, 86
Cold War, 78
Coleman Bridge, 17–19, 45, 129
Coleman, George Preston, 129
Coleman's Mill, 35, 183
Collector of Customs, lower James, 14–15, 33
College Creek, 36
College of William and Mary, 3, 14, 33, 35, 38, 80, 81, 96, 107, 120, 133, 140
Colonial dining, 161–163
Colonial inns, 161–163
Colonial National Historical Park, 17–19, 120–121
Colonial Williamsburg Magazine, 17

Comanche Indians, 4
Company D, 4th Virginia Infantry, 76
Confederacy, 61–64, 181–184
Confederate navy, 71–72
Confederate navy yard, 71
Coolidge, Calvin, 115–118
Copeland Park, 123
Copeland, Walter Scott, 115–118
Cornwall, England, 20
Cornwallis, Lord, 17–19, 32, 41–44, 182
Corotoman River, 11
Covered Wagon Association, 109–111
Crabs, 137–139
Crab pots, 185–187
Craney Island, 27, 48, 51–53
Crisfield, Maryland, 80, 81
Croakers, 137–138
Crossley, Red, 119, 133, 137
Crumpler, Weymouth, 99–100
Crutchfield, Stapleton, 51 53
CSS *Virginia,* 71
CSX rail company, 147–148
Cuba, 76–78
Cunard-White Star Line, 147
Curtiss engine, 112
Curtiss, Glenn, 99
Custis mill, 35, 153

Daily Press, 71, 77
Dalton, John, 152–154
Darling, James S., 85–87, 168
Davis, Donald, 108
Davis, Jefferson, 66–67
'Day boat,' 74, 101–103
de Bernardi, Mario, 113
Declaration of Independence, 158
Deep Creek, 27
Degen, Horst, 152–154
de Grasse, Admiral, 32
Delft tiles, 19
Delk, O.G., 84
Deltaville, 106–108
Denbigh plantation, 183
Democrats, 58
Depression, 118, 139
de Silvestre, Antonio, 15
Dickens, Charles, 107
Dimmock, Charles, 179
Dinwiddie County, 4
Dirigibles, 112
Dismal Swamp, 23–29
Dixon, Thomas, Jr., 91–93, 180
Doolittle, Jimmy, 112

Douthat family, 73
Downing's *Indian Wars,* 15
Dozier, J. M. 69–70
Drewry's Bluff, 71
Duke, Charles J., 108
Duke, Maurice, 11, 13
Duke of Gloucester Street, 34
Duke of York Motel, 107
DuPaul, William, 165–166
duPont, Samuel, 62
Dutch privateers, 33

Eagle population, 188–190
Eagle Point plantation, 179
Eaker, Ira, 122
Earthquakes, 88–90
Eastern Shore, 167–169
Eastern State Hospital, 107
Eclipse, 84
Eel fisheries, 164
Eisenhower, Dwight, 123
Elizabeth City County, 37, 68
Elizabeth City, North Carolina, 28
Elizabeth River, 25, 27
Elisha Lee, ship, 169
Elmington plantation, 91–93
Ely, Eugene B., 99, 100
England, 14, 32–34
Epes, Charlie, 86
Ewell, Benjamin, 66, 67
Excursion trains, 86
Exmore, 167

Farming, 149–151
Farragut, David, 64
Fauquier, Francis, 108
Federal Wildlife Refuge, 29
Fendall-Lee House, 158
Ferguson Park, 123
Ferguson's Wharf, 74
Ferries, 140–142
Ferry at Charles City, 6
Fiat airplane, 112
First Provisional Air brigade, U.S. Army, 104–105
Fishing, 177–179
Fitzhugh-Lee house, 159
Fleet, Betsy, 7
Fleete, Henry, 7, 10
Fleete's Hill, 10
Fleiss, Heidi, 125
Flippo, Ray, 162
Flying Fortress, 122
Ford, Henry, 96
Fort Algernon, 181

Fort Calhoun, 54–56. *See also* Rip Raps, Fort Wool
Fort Crafford, 16, 70
Fort Eustis, 15, 68–70
Fort George, 162
Fort Magruder, 66–67
Fort Monroe, 27–28, 50, 54–56, 65–67, 154
Fort Sumter, 61
Fort Wool, 55, 56. *See also* Rip Raps, Fort Calhoun
Foster, Lucille, 108
Four Mile Tree plantation, 102
France, 20–22, 41–44
Francis Street, 51, 58
Franklin, Benjamin, 16, 189
Franklin, Virginia, 24
Fredericksburg, 62
Freeman, Douglas, 70
French Line, 147
French privateers, 33
'Frenchman's Map,' 129
Friendship Fire Engine Company, 159
Fulton, Robert, 74
Funch, Edye, & Company, 146
Furs, 10

Gable, Clark, 122
Gadsby, John, 162
Gadsby's Tavern & City Hotel, 157, 161
Gainer, Earl, 109–111
Galveston hurricane, 143
Gardiner, David, 58
Garrett, Van, Jr., 108
Gay Manufacturing Company, 24
Gay, Texanna, 24
Gay, William H. 'Pappy,' 24
Geddy, Thomas, 108
George Washington Memorial Park, 127
'Gibraltar of the Chesapeake,' 176
Gilmer, Thomas Walker, 57, 58
Glasgow, Scotland, 32, 34
Glass House Point, 128, 141–142
Gloucester County, 20, 38, 61, 62, 106, 144, 164–166
Gloucester regiment, Virginia militia, 61–62
Gloucester Town, 11, 17–19, 144
Golden Flyer, 99
Goodwin's Island, 12
Gosport Navy Yard, 51
Government Dock, Old Point, 167–169

Governor's Palace, 39
Grandview, 86, 120, 158
Grant, Ulysses S., 163
Graves, Captain, 75
Gray's Creek, 103
Greate Roade to the West, 128–130
Great Britain 20–22, 112–114
Great Bridge, 26–29
Greenspring plantation, 36, 128, 182
Grist mills, 35–37
Green, Bennett, 149–151
Greenway plantation, 58
Griesenauer, Paul, Sr., 35
Griffith, David Wark, 91
Guinness, Alec, 56, 153–154
Gulf Coast, 54
Guittar, Louis, 15, 33
Gulf of Mexico, 4, 64
Gwaltney, P. D., Sr, 84

Halfway House, York, 182
Halifax, North Carolina, 28
Hall, John Lesslie, 108
Halsey, William F., 159
Hamilton, Katherine Withers (Mrs. Philip W.), 178–180
Hamilton, Philip W., 178
Hampton, 14, 27, 51–53, 68, 76, 85–87, 167–169, 181–184
Hampton Channel, 154
Hampton Creek, 51–53, 138, 181–184
Hampton Monitor, 71
Hampton Parish Church, 182
Hampton River, 14, 27, 54–56, 62–64, 94–96, 99, 106, 112–114
Hampton Roads Bridge-Tunnel, 54, 130, 154–155
Hampton Roads ferry, 112
Hampton Roads Port of Embarkation, 124
Hampton University, 33, 85
Hargis, William, 19
Harper's Illustrated Weekly, 27
Harrison, William Henry, 57
Harrison's Landing, 71, 74. *See also* Berkeley plantation
Harvey, Sir John, 8
Harwood family, 73
Harwood's mill, 37, 183
Haughwout, Mrs. J.M., 108
Havre de Grace, Maryland, 51, 53
Hazzard, David, 14
Henrico County, 71
Henry Fleete, Pioneer. etc., 17
Henry, Patrick, 107, 163

Herbert, Mrs. Mary Ann Dobbins, 85
Hewins, Charles, 85
Heymann, Peter, 14, 33
Heymann, Sir Peter, 14, 33
Hiden, Philip W., 115–118
Hilton Village, 137
History of the Dividing Line, 23–29
Hitler, Adolf, 155–156
HMS *Betsy,* 41–44
    Charon, 42
    Narcissus, 48–50
    San Domingo, 41–44
    Shoreham, 33
Hodges, Courtney, 123
Hoffman, Allan, 146
Hog Island, 102
Hoke, Kremer, J., 108
Holland, Robert, 109
Holland-America Line, 146–147
Host, T. Parker, 146
Hotel Warwick, 118–119
House of Burgesses, 17
Howard's Mill, 37
Hunley, Mary, 62
Hunt, Reverend Robert, 35
Hunt's Mill, 35
Hunt, Thomas, 36
Huntington, Archer, 139
Huntington, Collis, 62–68
Huntington Rifles, 76
Hurricane Agnes, 88, 143–145
Hurricane Camille, 143
Hurricane David, 143
Hurricane Hazel, 143
Hurricanes, 88–90
Hussey, Woodroof Hiden (Mrs. Wendell), 115–118
Hygeia Hotel, 28, 181

'I Cover the Waterfront,' 79–81, 131–133
Imperialism, 76–78
Indian fur trade, 10
Indians, 3–10
'Insane Asylum,' 107
Intracoastal waterway system, 24–29
Ice age, 4
Isle of Wight County, 82–84, 141–142
Isle of Wight Courthouse, 163
Italy, 112–114
'I Wanted Wings,' 122

Jackson, Andrew, 27, 55, 58

Jacobs, Eastman, 122–123
Jacques Schneider Trophy, 112–114
Jamaica, 16
James City County, 35, 68
James River, 3, 4, 5, 6, 14, 15, 33, 73–75, 82–84, 101–103, 131–133
James River Bridge, 82, 84, 115–118, 119, 138
Jamestown, 3, 7, 8, 13, 35, 74, 94, 96, 101–103
Jamestown Exposition, 94–96
Jamestown ferry, 141–142
Jamestown Festival Park, 172
Jamestown fortifications, 140
Japanese, 110–111
Jarvis, James, 51–53
Jefferson Avenue, Newport News, 100
Jefferson, Joseph, 178
Jefferson, Thomas, 89
Jeffrys, Lord George, 150
Jericho Canal, 24–29
John H. Kerr Dam, 4. *See also* Buggs Island Dam
John L. Roper Lumber Company, 29
John Tyler Highway, 128
Johnston, Joseph E., 62, 65–67
Jones, Hugh, 32
Jones, John Paul, 162
Jones, Reverend Ruffin, 108
Jones's Mill, 35, 183
Jones's Millpond, 35
Jordan, Samuel, 4, 5
Jordan's Point, 4, 5, 6
Juilliard Conservatory, 155
Juniper water, 28

Kale, Wilford, 17
Kane, Harry, 152–154
Kecoughtan Road, 129
Keith, Reverend George, 182
Kelly, Walter, 184
Kelly's Fort, 62
Kennedy, John F., 58, 162
Kennon's Mill, 183
Kent, England, 14, 33
Kent's Island, Maryland, 7
Key, Francis Scott, 162
Kilmarnock, 13
King Charles I, 7
King William and Queen Mary, 14
King's Arms Tavern, 161–163
Kingsmill plantation, 102
Kirby, Mary Ware Galt (Mrs. V. Lee), 108

Kitty Hawk, North Carolina, 99
Klaw and Erlanger theaters, 178
Kortkamp, Moreland, 155–156
Krogstad, Arnold, 122

Labor Day, 85
Lafayette, General, 55, 163, 182
Lake Drummond, 44–49
Lake Matoaka, 36
Lake Maury, 119, 139
Lancaster County, 10
Lane, Henry, 61, 62
Langley Field, 104–105, 122–124
Langley Memorial Aeronautical Laboratory, 104–105
Lanier, Karl, 86
Laurel Brigade Inn, 161–163
Lay, Beirne, 122
Lay, Ludwell Lee (Mrs. Beirne), 122
Leal, William, 94 96
Lee, Henry 'Lighthorse Harry,' 26, 157
Lee, Martha, 69
Lee, Richard Decatur, 68–70
Lee, Robert E., 8, 55–56, 65–67, 154
Lee, S.P., 71, 72
Lee, Thomas W., 70
Lee, William, 68–70
Lee Hall Manor, 68–70
Leviner, Betty, 38
Lewis, B.F., 185
Lewis, Fielding, 26
Lewis, John L., 159
Lewis, Lawrence, Jr., 23
Library of Congress, 26
Life on the Mississippi, 71
Lincoln, Abraham, 55, 61–67
Little England plantation, 181
Lively, Virginia, 13
Liverpool, 32
Lloyd House, Alexandria, 158
London, 32, 24
Longfellow, Henry Wadsworth, 28
Lord Baltimore, 7
Louisiana, 7
Loy, Myrna, 122
Ludwell, Philip, 36
Ludwell's Mill, 183
Luning, E. D. J., 146
Luray, ship, 84
Lynnhaven Roads, 21, 22, 32

Macomber, Susan, 115–118

Macon, Georgia, 99
Madagascar, 15
Madame Rose's Dream Boat, 127
Magnuson Act, 76
Magruder, John B., 62
Maine, The, plantation, 36
Manila Bay, 110
Mansfield, Richard, 179
Mapp, G. Walter, 131–133
Marine Corps, 112
Mariners' Museum, 44, 119, 129, 139, 144
Mariners' Museum Journal, 46
Mary Ball Washington Museum, 11
Maryland, 10, 79–84, 131–133
Maryland, ship, 169
Maryland Eastern Shore, 45
Mason, George, 158
Mason's Ordinary, 157
Mathews, County, 20–22, 45–47, 106–108
Mathews, Samuel, 183
Mayflower, yacht, 74–76
McCary, Ben, 3
McCauley, Charles, 63
McClelland, George B., 55, 56, 62, 65–67, 129
McMenamin crab house, 168
Mercury Boulevard, 109, 130
Methodists, 45
Mexican War, 55
Middle Peninsula, 45–47
Middle Plantation, 36, 128
Middlesex County, 20–22, 106–108
Middlesex County court, 22
Middleton, Reverend Pierce, 32, 129
Miles, Nelson A., 77
Milford Haven, 20
Mill Creek, 168
Mine warfare, 153
Mississippi River, 64
Mitchell, Marjorie, 155–156
Mitchell, William ('Billy'), 100, 104–105, 114
Mobilian Indians, 4
Mobjack Bay, 45–47, 168
Model T Ford, 85, 96, 106–108, 129
Mongols, 3, 4
Monroe, James, 50, 54, 56, 154
Monroe Doctrine, 76–78
Monticello, 89
Monument Lodge, 107

Moore, Gay Montague (Mrs. Charles Beattie), 157
Moore, Tom, 23, 27
Moses, 4
Moton, Robert R., 85
Mount Vernon, 26, 157
Mulberry Island, 16, 68–70, 74, 149, 182
Mussolini, Benito, 112
Myers, John, 52, 53

'NACA nuts,' 122, 123
Nansemond River, 24, 25
National Aeronautics Administration, 104, 105
Natl. Air & Space Museum, 100
Natl. Endowment for the Humanities, 43
Natl. Geographic Magazine, 44
Natl. Oceanic & Atmospheric Administration, 41
Natl. Park Service, 3, 35, 120–121
Natural Bridge, 23
Nature Conservancy, 23–29
Naval Institute, 109
Naval Operating Base, Norfolk, 112
Navy Torpedo Factory, 160
Nelson, Earl, 80, 133
Nelson, Thomas, 26
New Kent, 8, 66, 67
New Kent Stage Road, 129
New Map of Virginia, 22
New Mexico, 3
New Orleans, 64
New Point, 45–47
New Point Light, 45–47
New York, 64
New York Shipyard, 111
New York Times, 80
New York World, 99
Newport News, 59, 62, 70, 76–78, 83–84, 115–118, 146–148
Newport News Academy of Music, 178
Newport News bordellos, 25–27
Newport News city park, 173
Newport News Historical Committee, 99–100
Newport News Shipbuilding, 44, 76–78, 138
Newport News trolley line, 119
Newport News Times-Herald, 143
Newsome Park, 123
Niagara Falls, 23
Nicholson, Francis, 21–22

'Night boat,' 74, 101–103
Nimmo, Gershon, 26
Norfleet, Elizabeth Copeland (Mrs. Fillmore), 117
Norfolk, 26, 28, 34, 83, 92, 94–96
Norfolk County, 26
Norfolk Gazette & Public Ledger, 49–50
Norfolk Grays, 63, 64
Norfolk Herald, 55
Norfolk Naval Air Station, 153
Norfolk Naval Shipyard, 51, 55, 56, 63, 64
Norfolk Southern Corporation, 29
Norfolk spots, 138
North America, 3, 137–139
North Carolina, 10, 23, 24, 25
North German-Lloyd Line, 147
North River, 91–93
Northern Neck, 11–13, 46
Northwest Landing, 26
Norton, Randolph, 106–108
Norton Lilly & Company, 146
NYP&N transport line, 167–169

Ocala, Florida, 24
Ocean View, 144
Ocean shipping, 146–48
Ocean view spots, 84
Occoneechee Indians, 3, 4, 6
Occoneechee Town, 4
Ocracoke Inlet, 14, 16
Old Dominion Land Company, 67–70, 116
Old Dominion Steamship Company, 82–84
Old Point Comfort, 14–16, 45, 54–56, 76–78, 92, 104–105
Old, Robert, 122
Old Town Alexandria, 157–160
Olmsted, Frederick Law, 28
O'Neal, V.J., 176–177
Opechancanough, Chief, 10
Orcutt, Calvin, 116
Ospreys, 20
Outer Banks, 152–154
Ovid, 7
Oyster wars, 132–133
Oystering, 79–81, 131–133

Pagan River, 83, 84
Page, Governor John, 29, 40
Page, John, 38
Page, Mann, 38
Page, Thomas Jefferson, 61, 62
Page, Thomas Nelson, 40

Paine, William A., 115
Palace Green, 40
Palmer House, 66, 67
Parker, John C., 24
Parker, Colonel Richard E., 52
Pasquotank River, 27
Peachy, Bathurst Dangerfield, 108
Peachy, Muriel Bozarth (Mrs. B. D.), 108
Pearl Harbor, 110
Pembroke churchyard, 33
Peninsula Campaign, 44, 45, 54–67
Peninsula Guards, 76–78
Peninsula of Virginia, 14–16, 61, 62, 65–67, 119–121
Pennsylvania, ship, 161
Percy, George, 172
Petersburg, 10, 34, 163
Phi Beta Kappa, 140
Philadelphia, 27
Phillips, Owen, 27
Phillips, Sinclair, 125
Phillips, Thomas, 70
Phoebus, 78
Phoebus, Harrison, 182
Piankitank River, 45, 106–108
Pier A, Newport News, 74, 82, 84, 101–103, 119
Piracy, 14–16
Plantation on the James, 73–75
Plantain, John, 15
Plantation Flats, 167
Plymouth, North Carolina, 28
Pocahontas, ship, 75, 94–96, 101–103
Poe, Edgar Allan, 23
Point Breeze, Newport News, 146
Point Comfort, 14–16
Poquoson, 71
'Porte Crayon,' 27
Portsmouth, 29, 34, 51–53
Portsmouth Ditch, 29
Portsmouth River, 7, 57, 64, 88
Potomac Compact, 80–81, 132
Powell's Lake, 35
Powhatan, Chief, 5, 7
Powhatan Creek, 35
Powhatan Indians, 5
Powhatan Mill, 35
Powhatan Swam, 34, 36
Preserving wetlands, 172–174
President, ship, 22
Prince George County, 4, 6
Profiles in Courage, 58
Prostitution, 125–127
Puerto Rico, 79

Puller, John, 62
Purvis, George, 20–22

Queen Anne's Revenge, 16
Queen Anne's War, 16
Queen Street, Hampton, 181
Queenstown, Lancaster, 11–13

Raccoon Chase, 36
Ragged Island Wildlife Area, 173
Raleigh, Sir Walter, 32
Ramsey, William, 160
Randolph, John, of Roanoke, 142, 163
Rappahannock River, 11, 20–22
Reconstruction, 102
Red Fox Tavern, 161–163
Red Point, Smithfield, 147
Red Star Line, 147
Register of Virginia Historic Places, 19
Revolution Bicentennial, 19
Richmond, 65–67
Richmond Blues, 118
Richmond Enquirer, 52
Richmond Times-Dispatch, 35
Richmond Willow Works, 126
Rich Neck plantation, 36–37
Richter Scale, 89
Rip Raps, 44–48, 154–155
River Road, Newport News, 146–148
Roadways, 128–130
Roane's Wharf, 180
Roanoke River, 4
Robbins, Dorothy, 84
Robins, Joseph J., 62
Rochambeau, Comte de, 182
Rock crabs, 165
Rockwell, Norman, 107
Roller, Moreland (Mrs. Clyde), 155–156
Roma airship, 105
Romancoke plantation, 8
Rome, 4
Rommel, Erwin, 154
Roanoke River, 3, 6
Roanoke River Valley, 4
Robinson, John, 26
Rogerson, Isaiah, 28
Rolfe garden, 95
Roosevelt, Franklin D., 153
Roosevelt, Theodore, 76, 94–96
Roseland Manor, 182
Rosewell plantation, 38–40
Rouse, Randolph, 86

Route 5, Virginia highway, 35, 128
Route 17, 19, 46, 180
Route 60, 129
Rusk, Dean, 159

St. George's River, 7
St. John's Church, Hampton, 14, 51
St. Luke's Church, Smithfield, 12
St. Mary's White Chapel, 12, 13
Salem, North Carolina, 89
Salisbury, 5
Salter's Creek, 139, 181
Sampson, William T., 77
San Francisco Bay, 100
Sandbridge, 144
Sandy Point, 102
Sandys, George, 7
Savage, Fred, 108
Savage, Tom, 7
Savage, Toy, 24
Scallop dredging, 175–177
Schilt, Frank, 113
Schwarzkopf, Norman, 65
Schneider Cup Races, 112–114
Scotland Wharf, 74, 140
Scotch-Irish, 151
Seaford Scallop Company, 175–177
Seaplanes, 112–114
Seay, Captain, 119, 137
Seismological Observatory, 88–90
Seven Days' Battles, 66, 67
Severnby plantation, 178
Sewell's Point, 55
Shelby, North Carolina, 92
Sherwood Forest plantation, 58
Shewmake, Oscar, 108
Shields' Tavern, 163
Shirley plantation, 102–103
Shomette, Donald, 63
Shoreham, ship, 15
Short, William, 140
Silent Spring, 29, 188
Skiffe's Creek, 139
Skyways, 105
Smith, Doug, 139
Smith, Captain John, 3, 5, 164, 172–174
Smithfield, 82–84, 117, 141–142, 150–151
Smithfield Boat Line, 84
Smithfield ham, 161
Sniffen, Harold, 147
Snyder, William, 172–174
Soft crabs, 165, 185–187
Soldiers' Home, Phoebus, 77, 78

Southampton County, 24
South Carolina, 26, 43
South Mills, North Carolina, 27
Southside, 115–118, 140–142, 149–151
Spaatz, Carl, 122
Spain, 76–78
Spanish-American War, 76
Spanish fleet, 77
Spellman, Henry, 7
Spencer, J. B. C., 108
Spitfire planes, 114
Spotswood, Alexander, 16, 39
Spruance, Raymond, A., 123
Stabler-Leadbetter Apothecary, 159
Stanard, William G., 101
Squid fishery, 164
Stanley Hundred, 70
Stanton, Edwin M., 65–67
Storms, 88–90
Stowe, Harriet Beecher, 28
Stratemeyer, Robert, 122
Stretchley, John, 12
Strother, David Hunter, 27
Stuart Gardens, 123
Stuart, Jeb, 162
Submarines, 152–154
Submarine net, 124
Suffolk, 24, 26, 84
Sunday school picnics, 84, 85, 87
Sunderland, Archibald, 70
Surf bathing, 85–87
Surry County, 140–142
Surveyor, ship, 48–50
Swan's Point, 102
Sweet Briar College, 151
Swem, Earl Gregg, 24–25, 35, 108
Swem Library, College of William and Mary, 51

Tabb, Dr. John Prosser, 93
Taliaferro, William Booth, 61, 62
Tangier Island, 187
Tarleton, Banastre, 17–19
Taylor, Robert Barraud, 51–53
Teddington plantation, 182
The Approaching Storm, 153
'The Birth of a Nation,' 91, 180
The Clansman, 93, 180
'The Dawn Patrol,' 109
The Leopard's Spots, 93
The Life Worth Living, 91–93
The Site of Old James Towne, 1607–1698, 101
The Traitor, 93

Teach, Edward, alias Blackbeard, 14–16
'Test Pilot,' 122
Thimble Shoal light, 167
Thomas, Isaiah, 45
Thornton, John, 22
Thoroughfare, the, 96
Three Sisters, ship, 84
Times Herald, The, 115–118
Tobacco culture, 5, 32–34
Tobacco Coast, 32, 129
Tobacco fleets, 14–16
Tobacco ports, 17
Town Creek, 11, 13
Tracy, Spencer, 122
Trask, Benjamin, 46
Travis, Eddie, 86
Travis, Samuel, 48
True, Ransom, 73
Truxtun, William T., 71
Turner Construction Company, 118
Twain, Mark, 73
Tyler, John, 55, 57, 58, 154
Tyler, Julia Gardiner (second Mrs. John), 58
Tyler, Lettie Christian (first Mrs. John), 55, 57, 58
Tyler, Lyon Gardiner, 58
Tyndall's Point, 17, 129

U-boats, 152–154
Uncle Tom's Cabin, 28
Union Camp Corporation, 23–29
Union Chapel, Newport News, 116
University of Virginia, 149
U.S. Air Force, 104–105
U.S. Army, 54–56
U.S. Army Air Corps, 152–154
U.S. Department of Interior, 23–29, 43
U.S. Fish & Wildlife Survey, 188–190
U.S. Navy, 99–100, 109–111, 152–154
USO in World War II, 155–156
U.S. Shipping Company, 146
Upshur, Abel, P., 57, 58
USS *Birmingham,* 99–100
 Chocurra, 71
 Edsall, 110
 Jupiter, 109–111
 Kearsarge, 76–78
 Kentucky, 76–78
 Langley, 109–111
 Merrimack, 63, 64, 71
 Marblehead, 118

 Monitor, 62, 71
 Mount Vernon, 111
 Nashville, 77
 Pawnee, 64
 Pecos, 109–111
 Princeton, 57
 Whipple, 110

Valley of Virginia, 151
Vest house, 66, 67
Viancour, Dick, 86
Virginia Beach, 144, 152–154
V-E Day, 156
V-J Day, 156
Va. Bicentennial Comm., 100
Va. Canals & Navigations Soc., 126
Va. Comm. of Fisheries, 79–81, 131–133
Va. Chamber of Commerce, 118
Va. Commonwealth Univ., 5, 11
Va. Dept. of Historic Resources, 41–44
Va. Dept. of Transportation, 3, 5, 128
Va. Div. of Parks & Recreation, 120–121
Virginia Gazette, 34
Va. General Assembly, 10, 17, 21–22, 26, 28, 36
Va. Institute of Marine Science, 18–19, 42, 80, 81, 132–135, 164–166
Va. Landmarks Commission, 19
Virginia Lee, ship, 169
Va. Marine Resources Comm., 80, 81, 132–133
Va. Militia, 48–50, 61, 62
Va. Ports Authority, 148
Virginia Tech, 88
'Virginian Judge,' 184

Walker, Jim, 119, 137
Walker, Thomas, 26
Waller Mill, 35, 183
Waller Mill Park, 173
War of 1812, 48–50
Warden, Mrs. Bruce, 179
Warren, Sir John, 49 50
Warner, Augustine, 179
Warner, E.P., 112
Warner Hall plantation, 179
Warner, William, 186
Warwick Avenue, 125
Warwick Boulevard, 117
Warwick County, 68

Warwick Courthouse, 183
Warwick Machine Company pier, 3, 8, 119
Warwick River, 183
Warwick Town, 183
Washington, George, 11, 23–29, 42–44, 66, 67, 107, 157
Washington, D.C., 50, 53, 65–67
Waters Creek, 119, 139
Weaver, Walter, 122
Wells, William, III, 175–177
Weldon, North Carolina, 28
West Avenue, 79, 82
West Coast, 99
West Point, New York, 159
West Point, Virginia, 8, 43
Withers, Dunham, 179
Wolf, ship, 20–22, 46
Wolf Trap light, 20–22, 46
Wolstenholme Town, 11
Wool, John, 55–58
Work, Margaret Leal, 94–96

World War I, 55–56, 83–84, 100
World War II, 29, 109–111, 112, 119, 122–124, 125–127, 152–154, 155–156
Wright brothers, 99
Wrike, Peter, 61
Wyatt, Sir Thomas, 7
Wythe, George, 182
Wild game, 173
Wild pigeons, 174
Williamsburg, 27, 66–67, 68–70, 94–96
Williamsburg Lodge, 58, 76
Willoughby Spit, 54–56, 76, 99, 100
Wilmington, Delaware, 75
Wilson, Woodrow, 40
Wilton plantation house, 102
Winder, Levin, 84
Windmill Point, 10
Windward Towers, 119
Winged Defense, 105

Wise, Spencer, 167–169
Withers, Alfred, 178
Wythe, George, 182

Yeardley, Sir George, 70
Yeardley House, 95
Yellow fever, 77
Yonge, Samuel, 95, 96, 101
York County, 68 70
York Rangers, 71
York River, 17–19, 35, 38–40, 48–50, 106–107
York River State Park, 120–121, 173
Yorktown, 17–19, 32, 38–40, 41, 43, 61, 62–65, 67, 68, 106–108
Yorktown Coast Guard Reserve Training Center, 121
Yorktown Naval Weapons Station, 38, 68, 121